"How can we be still in a world that worships the gods of productivity? For many of us, rest feels like an illusion—a luxury with an impossible price tag. But it doesn't have to be this way. I'm so glad Jenny has penned a book that helps us navigate the counterintuitive journey toward rest and wholeness."

Addison Bevere, COO of Messenger International and cofounder of SonsAndDaughters.tv

"In today's society, we are all familiar with the busy life. Many, including myself, are constantly striving to *accomplish*, *achieve*, and *check the box*. It seems as if the days get fuller and fuller and go by faster and faster, and *rest* is very difficult to factor in. In fact, often it's considered a sign of weakness when chasing success and significance! Therefore, as the mother of three very active boys, the wife of a focused and driven husband, a successful business entrepreneur, and a church planter and pastor, I am so encouraged by this beautiful perspective. We all need to understand the beauty of resting in God and the strength of it! Health, peace, and joy will result in those who understand that sometimes our greatest battles are won by finding peace in him—for 'with us is the LORD our God to help us and to fight our battles' (2 Chron. 32:8 NIV)."

Diane McDaniel, cofounder and pastor of Bethel Dallas

"Jenny Donnelly is declaring a sound from heaven for this generation, a sound reverberating the hope and resurrection life found in Jesus!"

Leeland Mooring, four-time Grammy-nominated Christian recording artist

"This book is a must for anyone looking to find the calm in the middle of life's crazy twists and turns. As an entertainer, I can be filled with all types of anxiety. Jesus has the solution, and Jenny communicates the biblical solution for real peace and rest!"

Raelynn, country music artist

"I have had the beautiful privilege of not only reading the pages of this book after it became ink on paper but also observing this book in action in the life of Jenny Donnelly, who lives in a place of rest unlike anyone I have ever known. She can be in full motion and 'still' at the same time, and she has taught countless others to do the same—from around kitchen tables to gatherings of hundreds of women to standing on stages across America. Jenny is a living, breathing testimony of the life lessons she shares in these pages. At a conference, I heard Jenny say, 'Learn to work from a *place of rest!*' I immediately became a student and digested every word of *Still*."

Ann Hammock, cofounder of Restoration
Outreach Ministries, Warrior, AL

"Over the last several years, I have had the incredible honor to know Jenny Donnelly, her husband, Bob, and her amazing children. I have been personally transformed by the message in *Still* and have witnessed the powerful application of the principles revealed in this book. The pages of *Still* are like medicine to everyone suffering from terminal bedlam. Jenny's book was written from her personal experiences and penned with astounding candor. You will laugh and cry in the same paragraph as Jenny's unique style of storytelling brings you face-to-face with your own desperate need for rest. This book speaks to the real day-to-day struggles to discover rest and provides simple principles to live in rest in the loving arms of a great Father. If you are ready to find the still, quiet resting place in the middle of your storm, read *Still*. It may be the last book you will ever read from a place of chaos."

Dusty Hammock, pastor, motivational trainer,
entrepreneur, and author of *Dream Again*

"Jenny's insight on rest is powerful, real, and desperately needed today. In an era of noise and distraction, many have lost the supernatural power found only in supernatural rest. It is the same supernatural rest Jesus displayed when he slept in a boat during a raging storm while the natural-minded men were filled with panic, anxiety, and fear. Jesus could sleep because no storm existed inside him. Jenny brings a vital impartation of this truth, which will enable twenty-first-century believers to produce much fruit while never leaving the feet of Jesus."

Sandy Van Alstine, founder and president
of the Bellevue Company

"Who wouldn't want to live in the garden with Jesus rather than in chaos with the author of chaos? We applaud Jenny for finding her rest and sharing these principles so that we also may fulfill our God-given assignments."

Richard and Sherry Wright, business leaders

STILL

STILL

7 WAYS TO FIND CALM
IN THE CHAOS

Jenny L. Donnelly

Revell

a division of *Baker Publishing Group*
Grand Rapids, Michigan

Published by Revell
a division of Baker Publishing Group
PO Box 6287, Grand Rapids, MI 49516-6287
www.revellbooks.com

Printed in the United States of America

Library of Congress Cataloging-in-Publication Data
Names: Donnelly, Jenny L., 1974– author.
Title: Still : 7 ways to find calm in the chaos / Jenny L. Donnelly.
Description: Grand Rapids, MI : Revell, a division of Baker Publishing Group, [2020]
Identifiers: LCCN 2019017715 | ISBN 9780800737177 (pbk.)
Subjects: LCSH: Christian women—Religious life. | Peace of mind—Religious
    aspects—Christianity.
Classification: LCC BV4527 .D665 2020 | DDC 248.8/43—dc23
LC record available at https://lccn.loc.gov/2019017715

20 21 22 23 24 25 26   7 6 5 4 3 2 1

green press
INITIATIVE

For my incredible children

Hannah
Samuel
Esther
Eden
Mercy

My greatest desire for you is that you find yourself
in the thick embrace of God's love every day of your life—
living, breathing, and working from this place.
Stay seated in REST, in Christ,
and you will experience life to the fullest.

He offers a resting place
for me in his luxurious love.
His tracks take me to an oasis of peace,
the quiet brook of bliss.

Psalm 23:2

CONTENTS

FOREWORD

*R*est is a reset. There is nothing like a pause in the midst
of chaos to remember our priorities.

My dear friend Jenny has written an indispensable
book on the subject of rest. If you're anything like me, you
know that we must be intentional about entering into rest—
especially with all the demands that come with being a wife,
mother, friend, and follower of Jesus.

Jenny goes after the areas in our lives that steal our rest and
deprive us of our strength while at the same time providing
solutions that position us for rest recovery. Regardless of the
season of life in which you find yourself, rest is needed and is
available to you.

As Jenny boldly points out, rest is not just a physical act—it's
a posture of the heart. It's time for us to be at rest with who
we are and whose we are, because first and foremost, rest is
rooted in love—knowing we are loved without rival. Without
this understanding, you will constantly be restless—anxiously
comparing yourself to and competing with others. When you

are founded on God's eternal love, your heart will be quieted and assured that no one can take you out of his love or replace you because you have no rival.

Selah . . . pause, rest, and think about that!

I am thrilled that Jenny has written *Still*, because she encourages us—in the midst of chaos—to still our souls and to be present. It is there that we find God's presence and power. At times, we are going to lose our rest. Challenges come, tragedies hit, and we find ourselves coiled up in unrest. However, in a world of certain uncertainty, one thing is certain: Jesus is the same yesterday, today, and forever. His love for you is never ending. Precious daughter, never lose sight of the promise of your King, who welcomes us all: "Come to me . . . and I will give you rest" (Matt. 11:28 NIV).

Lisa Bevere, *New York Times* bestselling author;
author of *Without Rival*, *Adamant*, and *Girls with Swords*;
and cofounder of Messenger International

ACKNOWLEDGMENTS

*W*ithout my husband, this book wouldn't exist. Bob, thank you for being patient with me and giving me enormous amounts of space to explore all that God has called me to. Thank you for your unconditional friendship and belief in me.

Pauline Wick and Ann Hammock, thank you for your unique gift of attention to detail as you combed through every word with me.

Jeremy and Tiffanee Cummings, you have amazed me with your tireless service to be certain this message comes fully alive.

To all my friends who cheered me on, you were a source of strength and encouragement that showed up right when I needed it.

Laura Gallier, thank you for believing in the message and initiating my relationship with my literary agent, Don Jacobson.

Don, thank you for your trust, perseverance, and energy that helped make this book a reality.

Vicki Crumpton, my editor at Baker Publishing, you were a dream to work with, and I was greatly encouraged by your heartfelt engagement with me.

And to Jesus, I am grateful for this message and the invitation to share it. I love walking on water with you. Let's keep doing this.

INTRODUCTION

I woke up this morning with plans to begin writing this book and somehow "this morning" has turned into 7:24 p.m.

I am sitting in my running car in the dance studio parking lot. My nine-year-old daughter, Esther, gets out of her dance lesson in ten minutes. Two babies are fussing in their car seats. Mercy is whimpering, while Eden is screeching, "I want Daddy! I want to go to church!" Big. Bursting. Tears. My ears hurt.

I cave in. "We are not going to church. No one is at church right now. If you stop crying, I'll give you my phone."

Tears freeze on her face. "Okay." Incredible composure. This is a new child.

I hate that a phone will calm her down. Resisting the temptation to judge myself as a lazy or failing mom, I am grateful for the few minutes to type the words you are now reading.

This is my life.
And rest is found right in the middle of it.

PART 1

THE SEARCH FOR REST

1

TANGLED

Sitting on the edge of my bed, I stared at an enormous pile of hangers tangled up on the floor . . . and began to cry.

A week earlier, I had purged a bunch of clothes from my closet. The unwanted items went in one pile and the hangers went in another. I stuffed the clothing into garbage bags so I could take them to the donation center. However, the large pile of hangers, twisted into one another, sat on the floor for several days. Even though the pile was blocking my way to the closet, I simply stepped over it as if it didn't exist.

A week later, sitting on my bed, I came undone. There was that stupid pile mocking me. Twisted, tangled, too much for me. I could not bring myself to begin to unwind it. It had somehow convinced me that I was that tangled mess. Completely overwhelmed with no idea where to begin this daunting task, I cried and cried. I was so mad, frozen, and frustrated all at the same time. How in the world can a pile of hangers feel so big? Bigger than I am?

No, I wasn't eight years old. I was twenty-eight! I felt like an infant sitting there, helpless and overwhelmed. I was disappointed in myself for not being able to *simply pick up a pile of hangers*. I must be seriously flawed.

I didn't know it then, but this outburst wasn't about the pile of hangers. It was about a twenty-eight-year-old girl who didn't realize she had allowed her outside circumstances to rule her inside world.

It looks a bit like this . . .

Outside Noise	Inner Voice
The house is put together, so . . .	I am put together.
The house is a wreck, so . . .	I am a wreck.
My spouse is happy with me, so . . .	I am happy with me.
My spouse is upset with me, so . . .	I am upset with me.
My project is on a tight deadline, so . . .	My joy is dead until this project is done.
My kids are screaming, so . . .	My head is screaming.

Shallow Answers

If you would have told me back then that I was experiencing bouts of unREST, anxiety, or moments of depression, you would have offended me. I am a woman full of faith! I read my Bible regularly. I pray. I exercise. I eat healthy. I am a successful businesswoman. I have an amazing husband. We love our kids. We have some good stuff going on in our lives, people! There was no way I could be one of "those people" struggling to cope with everyday life. Words such as *depression* and *anxiety* were for people who couldn't pull it together. Yet when I stared at that pile of hangers, I couldn't pull it together.

Fifteen years ago, I had all sorts of personal philosophies and opinions about how a person should deal with stress, depression, and anxiety. I am sad to admit that I viewed struggling people as primarily weak minded or weak in faith. Yet here I was, unable to put a pile of hangers away.

What do you do when an everyday life moment, like a pile of tangled hangers, becomes too much?

If you search online for "how to deal with anxiety/depression," you will get thousands of answers and reams of advice, each promising relief. You can try legal and illegal things, many of which cause secondary issues.

When I was working as a dietitian in a hospital, I would see people for weight loss. One of my patients said that she went on antidepressants and initially felt better. After some time, though, the side effect of weight gain from the medication snuck up on her. Consequently, she now felt more depressed than when she started taking the medication because she felt so bad about her body. She ended up back where she started, but worse. Cat chases tail. That is what I've been observing in our culture: people use solutions that don't ultimately get to the root of the problem and cause secondary issues.

The Root of UnREST

If we want to solve a problem, the most efficient way to get to the root is to ask, "What is causing this?" If we ask, "What will make me feel better?" we will probably end up with a temporary fix only to find that the problem soon resurfaces.

Let's say that every time I go to the dentist I have multiple cavities. I can continue getting them filled, but a good dentist will address what is causing the cavities and will teach me how to keep sugar off my teeth and gums. That is the root problem. Relying on a tooth filling as a "solution" will not prevent future cavities.

It's the same with preventing anxiety and unREST. If we want to solve the issue in our lives, we have to get to the root, not just "get a filling" as a temporary fix every time the issue rears its ugly head.

As I look around at all the solutions being offered for anxiety, I mainly see a lot of "fillings." I am an advocate of getting physical exercise, eating healthy food, taking quality supplements, using essential oils, engaging in a positive community, getting quality sleep, using breathing techniques, and taking time to pamper ourselves. Tools such as these to soothe anxiety can absolutely help a person who is spinning out of control. But do any of these deal with the root cause of anxiety? Are we aware of what is causing us to feel anxious?

Why is it so difficult to get to the root of a problem? *Because the root is underground.* We can't see it! We see the branches (the symptoms) and can come up with many techniques for chopping down the branches, but branches grow back. I love what Henry David Thoreau once wrote: "There are a thousand hacking at the branches of evil to one who is striking at the root."[1]

The root of unREST is likely invisible to you and the people around you. Most people think their anxiety, depression, or unREST is caused by their circumstances. Yes, life can throw us serious curve balls. Adversity is a guarantee if you are a citizen of earth. Yet there are hundreds of thousands of people who are anxious or depressed who do not have circumstances to match their level of unREST (i.e., tangled hangers). On the flip side, many people with extremely intense life circumstances are able to live without the torment of anxiety or depression.

In the chapters ahead, we will identify both the root of unREST and the ways to eliminate it. You can have REST. You can be still even in the middle of chaos.

2

CHAOS

*O*ur previous home had an old barn on our property that was built in the early 1900s. When we moved in, the barn was in similar condition to its original state—wood plank walls and no insulation. Our vision for the barn was that it would become a gathering place.

We had our first gathering the year we moved in on New Year's Day—it was absolutely freezing outside! I'll forever have the image of nearly sixty of us crowded around a furnace layered in beanies, scarves, and winter coats. Brrr! The inside temperature was nearly identical to the temperature outside.

Over the next several months, my husband and some friends renovated the barn. They installed insulation, Sheetrock, and heating and cooling. My very gifted friend Kelly designed the interior with comfort and warmth in mind. She filled the rooms with cozy furniture, soft couches to sink into, and beautiful hanging chandeliers.

Because of these upgrades, our barn gatherings became events at which people would throw off their coats in the winter and come indoors to cool off in the summer. The inside temperature of the barn was no longer at the mercy of the outside weather. The cracks were covered and the temperature set to our liking. If it was freezing outside, it didn't affect the inside. If it was blazing hot in the middle of the summer, the air-conditioning unit allowed us to REST peacefully inside this space.

Like the barn, we all have an "outside temperature" and an "inside temperature." Let me explain. Outside weather conditions are things happening around us—relationships, jobs, families, health, the condition of our homes, and so on. Inside weather conditions are determined by our spirits and our souls—our minds, wills, and emotions.

Some of us live our lives in a similar condition to the old barn. We have cracks and openings everywhere. The weather outside billows right through to our insides, determining our inside temperature, influencing our minds and ruling our thoughts.

Within every lifetime, harsh weather happens. Kids scream. People die. Jobs end. Relationships collapse. People hurt us. We hurt people. Storms happen. Trouble swirls all around.

When these things happen, how do they affect your inside life? Do circumstances like this set your inside temperature? Do you decide how you are going to feel, or do other people decide? If chaos is happening around you, does it make its way inside you?

Hiding from Life

In the comedy *Moms' Night Out*, the main character's husband arrives home from work. The house is a total disaster. The kids have wrecked it top to bottom. He calls out for his wife, looking everywhere around the house, and finally finds her tucked in their bedroom closet with a bag of chocolate.

He delicately says, "Hey . . . what happened?"

"Just taking a little break . . . Mommy time."

"Okay," he responds sweetly.

Holding up the empty bag of chocolate, she says, "I ate the whole bag."

"Ya? That's okay." He kneels down beside her, trying to hide his shock. "The whole bag?"

"Actually, I'm hiding," she admits with a sigh.

"From what?"

Her expression drops, and she sighs again. "The house."[1]

This is my favorite scene in the movie. It made me laugh hysterically because I could totally relate! Hiding and ignoring my outside life were my go-to pain meds (and if I don't stay aware, they still can be).

Hiding comes in many forms: distracting ourselves with work, avoiding people, making up excuses, and lying. We can even hide behind our beliefs or religiosity.

We can be fooled into thinking that if we don't make eye contact with our circumstances, then we won't have to feel their woes on the inside. We imagine we can close our eyes, cover our ears, and ignore what is going on so we don't have to feel the pain. Sadly, when we come out of our closets, or wherever we've been hiding, the house is still a disaster. The job is still stressful. The marriage is still frustrating. The teenager is still depressed. You get it. The outside is under attack, and without REST, our insides are as well.

REST Is on the Inside

What image pops up in your mind when you hear the word *REST*? Do you think of relaxing with your family, vacationing on a beach, curling up with a good book, or maybe napping? Those are all forms of REST, and I would say that most of us would automatically think in that direction. But what I want to do is take you into an entirely different dimension of REST, which surpasses all other forms of REST.

The kind of REST we are after has nothing to do with what we are *doing*. The REST I'm speaking of is not a verb. It is not the *act* of resting. This is critical to understand before we go any further: the REST that will change your life is deeper than what you are doing and completely disconnected from the condition of your life circumstances. This REST we are in search of is a *place*.

Did you get that? It is somewhere you *live*. Let that sink in. When you see the word *REST*, I want you to think of a place where you have decided to live from and remain in night and day, no matter what. This place is special. It is available to everyone and yet few know it exists.

It is critical to understand where REST exists: REST is an *inside* place. It exists *within* you.

I have prayed for hundreds of people over the last sixteen years, and many asked for their circumstances to change. This is a wonderful prayer, and I believe that God wants us to lean on him for everything. But I want to point out that rarely do people ask for prayer for their own hearts to change. Few of us ask for prayer for our insides. We pray for other people's insides but not our own. "God, pleeeease change them!" I wonder what would happen if we begged God to change us with the same desperation we ask him to change someone else?

3

LOST

I t's a parent's worst nightmare to lose their child in public. My oldest daughter, Hannah, just three years old at the time, came with me into the airport bathroom. As we were leaving, she stood right next to me as a large rush of people filled the terminal. People moved in all directions.

Before stepping out from the bathroom to merge into the crowd, I reached down to grab Hannah's hand and SHE. WAS. GONE. I panicked. "Hannah! Hannah!" My eyes darted left and right. I knew she had walked out without me, but I couldn't see through the sea of people. I ran one direction and then another, yelling her name over and over. Not a single person stopped walking, and my head felt as if it was spinning. I turned in several circles, and horrible thoughts flashed through my mind. I glanced up ahead of the crowd and saw her walking confidently in her own determined direction. She seemed to have no idea that she was headed the wrong way—without me! I ran up and calmly picked her up, hoping she hadn't realized she had been alone. This entire scene lasted about fifteen seconds, but it felt as if time stood still.

I asked Hannah, now seventeen, if she remembered that moment.

"Yes! That was so scary. I remember following someone out of the bathroom who I thought was you."

You've probably experienced this yourself. Maybe you got separated from your mom or dad as a kid or you couldn't find your own child. We *all* have the same reaction: fear.

What about an infant who gets dropped off at day care, or the reaction of your little one when you hand them to the babysitter? Many times the reaction is based on fear . . . fear of being left alone or being lost. With you, they feel safe (love). Without you, they feel lost (fear).

Separation Anxiety

You've probably heard of separation anxiety. This is considered normal for a child under two years of age. Over time, though, they begin to realize they don't have to worry or be anxious because Mom and/or Dad returned every time. They develop trust.

After the age of two, separation anxiety isn't considered a normal stage of development. It's considered a disorder because by now the child should know that their caregiver is coming back. Something is out of order in their mind, and fear has invaded their insides. They don't have the assurance that they are protected unless they are with the person to whom they are most attached (commonly their mother).

Separation anxiety does not apply only to children. According to *Psychology Today*, "Separation anxiety refers to excessive fear or anxiety about separation from home or an attachment figure. The diagnosis is now categorized as an anxiety disorder that can be present at all stages of life."[1]

With this in mind, I want you to consider this: you were God's idea. He borrowed your parents to get you here. He offered them the privilege of raising you. Maybe they did a good job at that. Maybe they didn't. Maybe they tried their best. Maybe your dad went to the store and never came back. Maybe your mom or dad died when you needed them most. Maybe you lived with multiple adult figures. Maybe you were an orphan.

But aside from your parents, I want you to think about this: you are not just a ball of skin and bones. You have a spirit. You have a soul. There is something more inside you than just a random combination of cells and tissue. Your earth suit—your body—houses your spirit and your soul. These are your "insides."

You are not just the result of a male and a female who had sexual intercourse. Your earth suit physically came from them, but where did your spirit and your soul come from? Who made those parts of you?

People answer that question in different ways, but I believe that what the Bible says is 100 percent truth. The Bible says that you were "fearfully and wonderfully made" (Ps. 139:14 NIV) and that God's number one purpose for creating you was so that he can have a sincere relationship with you. You are the apple of his eye. The very same God who made you and loves you is the One who created the ground you walk on, the mountains that catch your breath, the sunset that warms your heart, and the ocean that roars its power. We don't need to feel anxious because God made us, loved us, and planned good things for us to do before we ever arrived on the planet. The Bible states many times that his plans for us are good, and his desire is to have a genuine father-child relationship.

I Want My Mommy

Yesterday after church, I was holding my daughter, Eden, and she began whimpering and clinging to me because she wasn't feeling well. As I was chatting with a few people, holding her on my hip, an adult asked if they could take her to help me out. Eden would normally be happy to go to another adult, but not this time! She whipped her body away from them and buried her face into my shoulder. Her body language said, "I only want my mom." I thanked them for offering but knew Eden needed me for comfort. If you're a parent, I bet you've experienced this more than once.

In a similar way, my friend's two-year-old vomited at our house a few nights ago, and we all went rushing to help her. I looked at her and said, "Oh, honey, are you okay?" She pressed her eyebrows together and looked at me as if to say, "You're not my mom. I'm not impressed." She wanted her mom because Mom is better than someone "like Mom." This reaction isn't learned. It is innate in every child to want their real mommy or daddy in a time of stress.

Then something interesting happens in early childhood. We begin to feel the shame from our sin and turn away from the one who can comfort us. Every one of my kids demonstrated this desire to hide in shame when they got to an age when they realized they had pooped their diaper. Obviously, this is not an example of sin, but the awareness of "I just did something yucky" causes little ones to hide in shame so as not to be caught in this state. Hiding behind curtains, crawling under a table, and running to another room were all normal signals that it was time to initiate the potty training process.

If you're a parent, you also know that kids hide things behind their little backs and run away when they do something wrong. They steal a toy from a friend, and their sin nature doesn't want you to find out they did it. Sin certainly doesn't lean into correction. It's not long before every human yields to their sin nature and automatically turns away from their caretaker. Sin separates us from love and comfort. Anxiety abounds in this state of separateness.

This "turning away" follows us into our adult lives and amplifies the separation anxiety. We may have a head knowledge that Jesus paid for our sins and we are forgiven, but if we haven't run into the chest of God with our sin, we are not getting the comfort and love we need. When we encounter comfort and love from God himself, we can't help but be changed by it. His love changes us. We can be all-star Christians, serving in church, speaking, leading Bible studies, and still be turned cockeyed from the love of our Father. Why do we do this? Because we don't have the deep down confidence in his mighty, all-consuming, all-powerful love. We think he's hard. We think he's mad. We lower our eyes to the ground in shame because we haven't grasped how gloriously our sins were forgiven through the gift of Jesus Christ. When we read about the life of Jesus, we get to see the character of God, because Jesus said that if we've seen him, we've seen the Father. He is love. He is forgiveness. He is help. He is grace. He is mercy. He is correction. He is victory. He is Abba. He is the antidote to anxiety.

So if God is the primary caregiver of our spirits, souls, and bodies, wouldn't it stand to reason that we may feel anxious when even the slightest distress enters our day and we don't go to God as our primary comforter? As our parent? This genuine relationship with God means that we trust him with everything, especially the things we are ashamed of. Jesus died for full forgiveness of our sins so that we may go boldly to the throne of grace. We deliberately go to him to comfort us in times of need. He becomes our best friend, our guide, our coach, our nurturer, and our healer. Like a child who feels distress, we bury our face in his chest and turn away from false or temporary comforts.

Religion Is Not Comfort

Many people find throwing themselves at God in this very vulnerable way extremely risky. They don't want to call on God for comfort because they see doing so as "being religious," and they have been judged, condemned, or controlled by religious people proclaiming to be the godly elite. Others throw everything they have into religious behaviors in search of satisfaction that may come from "doing the right things for God" and somehow achieving a superiority by their religious disciplines. Both of these extremes are nowhere near the true comfort the Bible promises us through a real-life relationship with God.

Religiosity is not comfort. Attending church doesn't mean we have a genuine relationship with God. Religiosity is duty and it is bondage. Doing religious things is not comfort. The Spirit of the living God is comfort. He is a person and our Creator, and he is alive and present with you right now. If you would dare to offer your affection, your worship to God, you would find your face buried in his shoulder as you turn away from all the things that offer counterfeit comfort.

I see people (even Christians) turn to almost everything but God when they are worried, distressed, or anxious. We go to our pseudo-gods—something that can temporarily comfort us—but they do not provide real comfort. I love getting a massage. (I think I could get one every day.) A trip to the day spa will help me REST my mind, but it won't give me the depth of comfort my soul needs. Only God can provide a pure hope that touches my deepest needs of comfort, love, direction, protection, and peace.

There's a Hair Ball in This Relationship

If you can admit you have a slight resistance to allowing God to be this close to you, you may be surprised by what I'm about to tell you. My personal experience with this resistance and the many transparent conversations I've had with others who were attempting to get closer to God indicate that the resistance is most often the result of unforgiveness.

The most important thing you can do right now is to pause and ask God to help you forgive your family and friends, especially for disturbing memories from your childhood. Most of us just move on and leave that trauma in the past. But where hurt has been unresolved, we can carry unforgiveness. Unforgiveness that is not dealt with becomes bitterness. Bitterness can grow into a nasty root that grows deep in our insides, making us miserable, bringing harm to our physical bodies, and eroding the quality of our relationships with others. Bitterness should never be tolerated because it is so destructive.

Asking you to forgive those who have hurt you may be asking a lot. I know that the abuse and devastation some have faced are unimaginable. However, unforgiveness is the blockage in the spiritual heart. It's the hair ball in the drain blocking the flow. As difficult as this may be, if you can release the unforgiveness from your heart, you will feel a freedom enter your being immediately. Forgiveness doesn't mean that what someone did to you was okay, and it doesn't mean you must reconcile with that person. What it means is that you are no longer going to hold the person captive in your heart. Open the prison door and say out loud, "I forgive _____ and release them from my heart." Do this for as many people as you need to.

It's also critical to note here that I don't know a single person who doesn't need to forgive themselves. God knew you wouldn't be perfect and that you would choose evil over good. That is why he sent his Son, Jesus, to die in your place as a payment for your sins. Forgive yourself and receive the forgiveness of Jesus. Then choose not to rehearse what God has already forgiven you for and live for what lies ahead, not behind.

My prayer is that God's true nature will be revealed to you and that his all-consuming love will heal your heart and reveal and restore your worth. I had some good ideas about God and others not so good. I had to allow him to reveal himself to me through his Word and through his presence. No other person could represent him any longer. People are flawed and cannot live up to the full capacity of God's love for us.

If you ask God to reveal his heart for you, he will. But here's a warning for you: if you ask with a sincere heart, the love gusher will come! He is all love, and his love for you is personal and powerful.

Created in His Image

The Bible says you were made in God's image: "So God created human beings in his own image. In the image of God he created them; male and female he created them" (Gen. 1:27 NLT).

Just like our physical bodies were made in the image of our biological parents, our spirits were made in the image of God. When you are loving and kind, it's because you have God's kindness spirit genes. When you are generous, it's because God is generous, and his spiritual DNA got passed down to you. Have you ever felt sad, excited, or angry over an injustice? You got that from your eternal Dad. Have you ever burst into laughter and your heart just felt light and refreshed? That's his image in you.

The Root Revealed

So let's go back to the topic of separation anxiety. Think with me here and consider your own spirit and soul when I ask you this: Could it be that we have separation anxiety—fear of being alone, having to protect ourselves, no reliable backup, no hope of comfort—because we are separated from the original Creator of our spirits and our souls? Are we like Hannah—lost in a sea of people without parental protection and connection in a spiritual sense?

Could it be that this is the underground root we can't see—a separation or disconnect from the One who made us? Maybe we even divorced this God and chose another to raise us, but our spirits and our souls are still deeply longing for our Creator.

This separation from God, the One who loves us most, is the root cause of our anxiety, stress, anger, depression, numbness, and sense of being overwhelmed.

Have you ever found yourself asking, even crying out, "God, where are you? Do you know me? Do you care? I feel so alone. I feel like it's all up to me."

What if you knew the God who *knows you* by name? What if I told you that he knows how many hairs are on your head right now? What if I told you that he knit you together in your mother's womb . . . that she was the blessed carrier of beautiful you? What if I told you that your spirit and your soul were handed off to her and then she grew an earth suit to encapsulate them?

What if I also told you that God desperately wants to parent you, walk with you, provide for you, guide you, and help you? How would your life be different if you knew you had the Creator of the universe defending you, loving you, growing you, and fighting your battles for you? I don't know a single person who wouldn't want that help from him.

I'm telling you this because it's the truth: you were made by the same God who formed the earth. Until you are able to know by experience that he is alive, present, and available, you will experience the separation anxiety—turmoil, fear, depression, unREST—that comes with living life as an orphan.

I want to help connect you to the true God who made you so that you can REST in his arms, his plan, his care. He is so near. The irony is that he is so close that sometimes we need help finding him. He can seem so far away. We can even feel as if maybe he's angry with us or disappointed in us. Or perhaps you think he has bigger problems to attend to than yours.

I get all that, but I want to tell you my story . . . about a girl who suffered extreme separation anxiety from God and couldn't find him—so he had to find her instead.

4

SAD

I was raised by young and loving parents. They told me about Jesus and that if I wanted to ask him to live in my heart, I could invite him in. I remember kneeling next to my grandmother's bed, probably when I was just three or four years old, and resting my folded hands and bowed head on the white lace coverlet. I asked this man Jesus into my heart and remember the absolute assurance that somehow this loving guy was now living in my heart. I imagined a little man just wandering around in my insides.

I have a few faint memories of attending church—sleeping on a wooden pew or scribbling on paper next to my mom to pass the time. I remember going with my mom and dad to their friends' house, and they would pray. I was extremely interested in the feeling I could sense in the room. I remember the room becoming thick—it's difficult to describe, but I could sense a heavy presence fill the room when they all got together. I felt safe there. I would go back and forth from playing with kids in one room to peeking into the thick room.

When I was seven, my parents divorced. They were so young and weren't equipped to work through some of the challenges that come with marriage. When they split up, I went to live with my mom. She was a great mom, but I desperately missed my dad.

I would visit my dad during the summer. I absolutely adored him and knew he was the best dad on the planet. It was hard to be there each summer because, from the first night I was lying in my bed, I knew how much I would miss him after I left. I would sob, knowing before long I would have to say goodbye and that it would be a long time before I would see him again since he lived in another state.

I needed my dad, and that affected me. It left a space that felt dark within me. "Sad" would be the best way to describe that spot. It became a wound I would cover and conceal so as not to infect other people.

When I was ten, my mom married someone I was frightened of almost every day. I wanted to physically hide from him, and I did. Hiding was my friend.

We didn't attend church. Still, I had a strong curiosity about Jesus. Despite my mom's own sorrow and bouts of depression, she must have felt my longing for God because she gave me a tiny New Testament. It was the kind that fit in the palm of your hand with microscopic print. I'll never forget feeling comforted that she was connecting with God, at least by giving me a Bible. The memories of the thick presence of God in those prayer meetings had left my mind, but my spirit must have remembered.

I was thirteen years old when my curiosity about Jesus became very strong. I wanted to know this man Jesus. Who was he and why was he so famous? Why did some people talk about him and others pretend he didn't exist? Some people called him an inspiring teacher but denied that he was God in the flesh. Some people used his name as a curse word. I found it interesting that there was so much debate about who he was.

My older sister had been given a children's Bible as a little girl. The picture of Jesus on the front cover captivated me. Even though I was in junior high, I was drawn to the illustrations. I loved looking at the pictures. With lofty aspirations of reading this book cover to cover, I opened it to Genesis. My eyes seemed to cross after a few paragraphs—my mind couldn't digest the words. I had no idea that the stories of Jesus were found in the New Testament books of Matthew, Mark, Luke, and John. After flipping through the picture pages, I shut the book and clutched it to my chest. I decided that the next best way to be close to Jesus was to sleep with the Bible. I did this a few times when I was really longing to know this mysterious man who had first made contact with me that day I knelt against my grandmother's perfectly pressed white coverlet.

I remember going to a few church services with a friend and a family member, but I didn't feel my insides leap like I hoped they would. These were very formal churches, and I didn't understand what the people on the platform were saying. Church was out of the picture for now. For me, Sundays were reserved for sleeping in, watching television, and catching up on whatever I had put off until the last minute.

But most nights I allowed my mind to drift off into a larger space. I would think about this mysterious God and wonder . . . Did he have a plan for my life? Was he out there? And was it possible he was thinking of me? I wanted to connect with God. I just wasn't quite sure where he was.

5

LONELY

My mom and stepdad divorced after a seven-year marriage, and shortly after, I went off to college. My stepdad was a high-stress, success-at-all-costs type of guy, so he did leave some good in my life by setting a standard of excellence in grades and behavior. I had no intention of partying or messing around. I was after impeccable grades and a successful career, and my mind was set on it. On campus, I was known as a girl who had her stuff together—this was my identity.

I joined a sorority and entered the crazy world of sixty girls living in one house. I was the good girl, so I gladly offered to be a designated driver to my newfound friends. I even found a church and felt that same thick presence that I had felt in my mom and dad's prayer meetings as a child. I loved the worship and began to read my Bible a little. I came to a place where I felt that God and I were running side by side. I was excited about who he was and that he could heal people, love people, and save them from their sins. I had moments when I knew he loved me, but then I would question why the God of the universe would love me.

After a year or so, I saw my friends get boyfriends, and I would happily celebrate with them. I'd take them to one party after the next as my good-friend duty. They looked like they were having a great time (which I learned soon enough was not the full story). I would tell people about Jesus and hope they would pursue him, but after a while, I started feeling quite alone.

Unfortunately, the loneliness began to pick at a little girl wound that I didn't know was still lingering. "Sad" was still there ebbing and flowing in low to high strength. The more I watched other girls being pursued by boys, and watched boys walk right past me, the more I felt Sad ooze its infection. I concluded that I was not pretty enough to be sought after. I was not skinny enough to be the girl who caught the attention of a boy across the room at a party. I was the dorky sober girl who waited in the corner or pretended to have an entertaining conversation with a completely drunk individual. After some time, I came to believe that being a good girl was making Sad more sad. If someone could love me, perhaps the pain would begin to subside.

"Sad" Gets Its Way

I tried my first beer, and it temporarily relieved Sad. It felt amazing to be drunk (until the next morning—that was brutal). I finally knew why my stepdad and my friends drank alcohol. I didn't have to feel irrelevant anymore. I didn't have to feel ugly anymore. I hated being shy and timid, and alcohol gave me the courage to talk to boys. Boys began to take notice of me when I was drunk. It felt good to be noticed. It felt good to be seen.

I stopped going to church because I figured that God would be upset if I partied one day and attended church the next. I wasn't sure how that all worked, so I stopped attending church altogether and figured that God and I would hang out without church. I had no idea how Sad would drive me to deception. It made my decisions for me. It caused me to leave all my values and goals. It demanded me to relieve its pain.

For the next few years, alcohol was my pain reliever. I arranged my life around getting drinks and couldn't imagine my life without it. Regret always dumped itself on me the day after, and I would sob and cry with a pounding headache. My insecurities would escalate after a drinking episode. Still, I kept going back to numb the pain. Alcohol was the only thing I knew that would make Sad quiet for a moment.

Irrelevant

One day, sitting on the staircase in my sorority, I had the thought, *I don't know why I need to be a virgin.* Drinking alcohol attracted the guys, and I liked that. It made me feel relevant, valued. I began hanging out with a rather popular guy, and sadly, I slept with him. Of course, I didn't feel like I thought I would. It wasn't a romantic moment of two people adoring and serving the spirits of each other, as sexual intercourse is designed for in a marriage union. I had no idea that sex outside of marriage would cause me to feel empty. I remember leaving his dorm room and walking back to mine. I just felt blah.

I knew that something valuable was lost that day, which surprised me because I didn't know I had anything valuable to lose. I didn't realize my virginity was valuable until I felt the void of it. It felt similar to losing an extremely expensive diamond ring that has been passed down from your grand-mother. But I didn't know what to do with the loss, so I decided to stuff the feeling.

Apathy became easy for me. Apathy would treat Sad with a dose of Novocain when it cried. This allowed me to keep moving forward without feeling too much pain. I would straight-up deny that I had any pain. I would have lied straight to your face, because I lied to myself. And unfortunately, I believed myself. A person with pain, in my mind, was weak. I became good at giving Sad Novocain so that painful things didn't hurt so bad, and I desperately didn't want to be one of those weak people who felt bad for themselves all the time. (I couldn't stand self-pity and still can't!) And just like apathy was a Band-Aid, drinking helped numb me momentarily.

I also used healthy things to keep the pain down: excelling at my grades, cheerleading on campus, and making a few lifelong friends. I had a résumé of reasons that could prove to myself that I was succeeding at life.

The day after I gave away my virginity I was in the student union studying with the guy. I glanced across the table and saw a piece of paper with a list of first names in a straight column. My name was at the bottom.

"What's that?" I asked.

"Oh, this?" he replied. "These are all the girls I took their virginity from."

And that was that. The joke was on me.

You would think I would have risen up in courage and cussed him out. But remember, my wound wasn't anger; it was Sad. Our unresolved wounds will always do the talking. Sad was peeled open further that day, like a wound being sliced with a dagger. My heart shriveled in pain, and I knew I was the idiot.

It wasn't love or value that he saw in me. I was his agenda. I had fallen for the idea that maybe I was sought after for what value I carried on the inside. But the hard truth was that I was no more than a vagina. Maybe that's too raw for some people to hear, but it was a fact. Once again, I was irrelevant. With his words, my insides shrank, and I felt as if I was an inch tall.

You would think I would have broken up with him, but I didn't. I slept with him a few more times because, in my mind, I was damaged goods. My identity had become "Irrelevant," and so what did it matter now? Of course, looking back, having been restored of my worth, I see it this way: I got a flat tire and pulled my car over. And since one tire was flat and I didn't know how to change a flat tire, I just slashed the other three. It makes no sense that I continued to let myself be used, but again, Irrelevant and Sad made my decisions for me.

Done

I remember around that time I was riding in the car with my mom during summer break. I was staring out the passenger window, numb, sharing a few quiet words. I mentioned rather nonchalantly, "I don't even know if I want to live anymore. There doesn't seem to be a point."

Her response shocked me. At the top of her lungs, she bellowed, "DON'T EVER SAY THAT AGAIN!" She was fighting back the tears and breathing heavily. I hadn't seen this side of her in a long time, if ever. She was like a lioness roaring at a deadly predator approaching her cub.

The only thing I remember about my emotions in that moment was that it felt good that someone was fighting for me, because I had not an ounce of fight for myself. I still didn't know what the point of my life was, nor did I suddenly have an awareness of my value. But her voice pierced the darkness that was twisting its way through my insides. I felt the heavy cloud blow away. I don't remember saying anything back. I didn't have anything to say because I was depleted. But her outrage over the thought of me taking my life revealed that I was somehow worth fighting for.

As I think back to that short (and oh, so long) season, I cry for that sweet little girl who wasn't out to live a rebellious life. She didn't want to rip her heart open and give her virginity away. She didn't want alcohol and hiding to be her friends. She wanted her life to matter. She wanted to be relevant. Like every human on the planet, she was simply looking for someone to love her. Sadly, she looked in all the wrong places. But very soon, her True Love would find her, and he would ease the sting of pain.

6

DARKEST BEFORE DAWN

I went out to the bars like so many other nights. I was standing at the bar, scanning the room to see if any boy noticed me. Each one was engaged in conversation with a girl who I concluded was prettier or skinnier than I was. I was standing alone, embarrassed and unwanted . . . again.

I don't know how I got home, but what I know is that when I woke up the next morning, I awoke to a black hole. I didn't want to live. I didn't want to die. I wanted to disappear—forever. I'd never felt this before. It felt like a vacuum sucking out everything within me and there was no bottom to the dark hole. My insides were literally void of feeling. There was no love. No drive. No life. No will to live. I had never known a person could feel infinitely hollow. Sad had taken over *all* of me. There wasn't a single part of me that could find hope. Not a single ounce. The depth of this black hole was never ending. It was so black.

I was terrified. I managed to yell out to my roommate, "Something is wrong with me! Help me!"

She came into my room, took one look at me, and said with a look of concern, "I don't know what to do." She looked over-whelmed and scared. I probably looked like death—and I'm not exaggerating. I felt the darkness of the demonic inside and entirely void of the presence of God. No thick presence. No presence whatsoever. You don't know what you have until it's completely gone.

I got out of bed, and I have no memory of the next several minutes. Suddenly, I found myself walking along a sidewalk and barging through the double glass doors of a church just off campus. I had never been in this church. I arrived in whatever I had slept in, and I'm sure I smelled like alcohol and smoke.

I needed Jesus. I realized I was lost. Just like Hannah at the airport, I was a little girl who had stepped out into an unfor-giving world without grabbing hold of God's hand. I had been swept up in the wrong current.

I saw a woman behind a desk, and she looked startled when she saw me. Maybe she had never seen a girl in her pajamas recklessly storm through the doors in the middle of the day in the middle of the week. She immediately walked me down a hallway to a gentleman sitting behind a desk. I was sobbing. I have no idea what I said. All I know is that after I said it, he reached around and put a cassette tape in a cassette player, pushed play, and left the room.

I sat there alone. A twenty-minute song told a story that was freakishly the same as my story but with a new ending. The part that gut punched me was when the boy in the story was wrapped in heavy chains. They were choking the life out of him. All of a sudden, a man came and began to unwind the chains from the boy. I felt an immediate sense of rescue as I sat in that chair, sobbing by myself. Then the unthinkable happened: this man began wrapping the chains around himself. I didn't understand why he would do that! This man was Jesus.

Somehow I just thought that Jesus was like a superhero who fought crime for the good of the earth, and because he was God, it wasn't that big of a deal. This story was too much for me to bear. In my mind's eye, I saw my chains of loneliness and being unwanted suffocate him. He took my Sad on himself. He took my alcohol, hangovers, sexual shame, guilt, self-hatred, bitterness, hurt, and torment on himself. It was horrible. He wanted to take it, and I let him. I needed a Savior! I needed saving from this incredible pain. I needed my real dad—God. I couldn't bear the weight of my guilt, shame, and sadness any longer.

I listened to the story as he died . . . as he lost his breath in my place. The sin that was killing me killed him instead.

Something supernatural happened. In that moment, I was free! I could finally breathe. The black void began to fill with light, and immediately I felt my spirit take a gasp of air. For years, I had felt as if my spirit was being held under water. Oh, but this breath . . . this breath saved me! My body filled with hope and love. I knew God had rescued me. This sad, deceived, and ignorant girl had been rescued by God, her Father.

When the gentleman came back into the room, I was crying with tears of relief. I asked, "Can you tell me the name of this song so I can listen again?"

He responded, "This moment isn't about a song. It's about you and Jesus."

His words pierced me. Twenty years later, I still didn't know the name of the song, but I had come to know the One who sang it to me.

Just a few months ago, a friend in my church texted me. "I think I found the song." I clicked on the link she sent me, and sure enough, that was it.[1] I remembered how urgently God met me in the black hole that day.

As for the man who selflessly helped me, I never saw him again. He remains unnamed and unknown to me. However, I am certain his name is known in heaven.

7

"SAD" GETS CLEANED OUT

*E*veryone knows what it feels like to get a wound cleaned out. A small paper cut stings, and the deep gashes are excruciating. I wish I could say I was a saint after that saving moment, but it was just the beginning of a relationship. It was the beginning of a wound being cleaned out. I began allowing myself to feel things: pain, joy, desperation, confusion. I had shut the doors to my emotions in an effort to survive life, so these were very scary doors for me to open.

The man who played the song that day in the church office suggested that I deal with the bitterness in my heart. I had no idea that I was bitter and that God wanted me to open the door and face it. I discovered that I was bitter toward some of the people in my life whom I perceived as abandoning and neglecting me. I would slam the door shut and deny that a pile of trash was rotting in that closet. Then God would stand by the door and gently ask me to open it again. He would wait, but he wouldn't move.

Forgiveness became the first cleaning session for my wounds. I was in denial that I had people to forgive. I even had to forgive myself. This forgiveness journey was long. You think you're going for a short jog only to find out you merged into a marathon.

I would stumble, and God would pick me up. I would get stubborn, and he would be patient. It took awhile for me to stop drinking to relieve the pain. I even had another toxic relationship with someone. I would forget at times how black the hole was and take it for granted that I wasn't in that hole anymore. These things wouldn't make their way out of my life until I went through a few more bumps and bruises. Apparently, I still believed some lies about how to stay happy and loved. God stayed with me, though, and kept wooing me night and day. He kept telling me how much he loved me. I wanted to believe that, but I had believed I was unloved for so long. My brain had to be washed of the lies. As we say about a cooking pan with burnt food, "This one is a soaker."

I finally gave up. I broke up with my boyfriend of two years and came to the end of myself. Rather than just be extremely fond of Jesus, I gave my life to him. "Here, it's all yours. In fact, I'm all yours." I finally crossed the most profound threshold of my life: I made him Lord.

Making him Lord is different from just believing in him. He became my everything. After college, I rented a basement room from a family in a city where I knew no one. I was totally alone. I had no friends. But this time things were different. I cherished the small room and being by myself. I distinctly remember one night looking into a full-length mirror that hung on the wall. I stared into my eyes, and from the sincerest place in me, I told God that I didn't want to find my love in another person. I wanted only him.

I don't know if I said this aloud, but I was boldly declaring in my spirit, "If I am forty-eight years old before I have a spouse, then so be it. I don't care about another person's love. I am marrying you." A line in the concrete was drawn, and I stepped over it with both feet.

This changed everything. I meant it from the deepest place in me. It wasn't just a plea to get out of feeling horrible. I truly turned my back on false love and lustful desires to find a spouse so I could use him as a remedy to relieve my loneliness. I looked in that mirror and said, "I do." Jesus had been my Savior up to that point, but now he was my Lord. I had dated Jesus, but now we were married. My eyes would gaze at no other lover. I decided that being single for the rest of my life was better than the past few years of completely damaging myself.

My affection would all be spent on him. I spent hours reading my Bible and worshiping him and thinking about him. Like a new bride, I became obsessed with him. He was all I wanted to talk about. I once had a desperation for him to heal my pain, and now I had a sold-out desperation for *him*. He was my new husband. Sad began to heal, and the dark cloud began to give way to light. My heart had never felt this light, this passionate, this alive!

I didn't know Bible lingo at the time, but I have since learned that this is called "lordship"—when someone makes Jesus the Lord and master of their life. He gets it all. He becomes the King on the throne, while I step down from being the god of my own life. I couldn't get enough of him. I went from placing my attention on my own flaws and pain to putting my affection on the person of Jesus Christ. There was a deliberate shift: from focusing on my problems to focusing on Jesus. I had no other friends in that foreign city, but I had the only friend I needed.

8

STRONGER

*I*ronically, I met my husband, Bob, just a month after standing in front of that mirror and making Jesus Lord. When he asked me to go to dinner with him, I was extremely hesitant. My heart was guarded for the first time. I had value in me, and I wasn't going to let it get stolen a second time. I already had a man. My response was, "I'm not looking to date anyone or play games. If you say you're going to call me, then call me. But I'm not looking to play games." My old nature was gone, and I was already wearing a wedding ring. Sad was too far into the healing process for me to jab at it again, so I was reserved and had no problem telling him that.

He said, "It's just dinner. Will you come with me tomorrow night? I'll pick you up at dinnertime."

I was perplexed. "When is dinnertime?" I didn't know at the time that his family had dinner every night at 6:00 p.m. Totally foreign to me was the idea that dinner had a specific time. My family ate when the food was there, or you just figured dinner out for yourself.

Dinnertime came, and Bob took me out. At dinner, I told Bob straightaway, with no hesitation, that I was completely in love with Jesus. He didn't know Jesus at the time. As I had done when he mentioned dinnertime to me, he looked at me as if he had no idea what I was talking about.

We started talking about what we believed and lifestyle and moral issues. He said, "I believe two people should live together before they are married. It just makes sense to test the relationship."

"Not me. That's the opposite of what I believe." I had zero hesitancy because I couldn't have cared less about making this guy feel good about me. This was the exact opposite of my old, dead nature.

I had spent a month emptying myself of every piece of me I could find. In turn, God had filled me up with him, his approval, and I was stronger than ever. In fact, I had never had this much resolve and this much disconnection from the approval of others. God's strength had filled my bones, and I was immovable.

Bob didn't know the mess I had been in just months earlier. The smoke was still rising off my burned-up bonfire of pain. No, no, no. He couldn't talk me into believing that two people should use each other to see if the shoe fit. I had played house with my last relationship, and my heart had ended up a shredded mess. This conversation was easy as pie for me. He had a theory, and I had experience. My experience trumped his theory.

That is how our relationship started, yet I was irritated because I found a place in my heart that was really fond of him. He was kind. He wasn't macho. He wasn't self-centered.

He was an extremely logical person, so I thought he had to understand this Jesus guy. However, he didn't jump on my Jesus wagon. Every time we were together, I would talk about Jesus. I remember that on our third or fourth date I said, "Now that you know there is a God and he is known through Jesus, you need to know there is a devil too." The look on his face said, "You're killing me." I kept teaching him what I knew about Jesus, but I came home one night and sat on my bed with an ache and desperation in my heart. I said, "God, I really like him, but only you can change his heart. I refuse to give my heart to anyone who hasn't given his heart to you. So here you go. He's all yours."

The dates continued, and sex was absolutely out of the question. The devil puts intense pressure on us to have sex before marriage—then becomes absolutely committed to preventing it once we're married. It was only a short time later that Bob made Jesus his Savior, and ten months after that first date at dinnertime, we got married. After a three-week engagement, we got married in my dad's backyard in Burnet, Texas. The wedding was a blur, but I remember the sweet moments of getting dressed, putting on my makeup, and waiting to walk down the aisle with butterflies flittering in my stomach. Right before taking my first step down the aisle, my dad leaned over to me, prayed for me, and looped my arm through his.

I walked down the aisle and married a man who would spend the rest of his life surrendering his needs to meet mine. And right there under the cool overhang on the porch, as a married girl—who once wore a cloak of loneliness and shame—I danced with my dad.

"Sad" Knocks on a Newlywed's Door

I was completely caught off guard. The first night back from our honeymoon, Bob wanted to go out with some guys. I was livid. I was so mad that I got out of bed and walked to the grocery store that was open late. Bawling my eyes out, I felt so rejected that he'd rather be with other people than me. When I checked out, the cashier asked me if I was okay.

"No! My husband left me for his friends." I was sad.

"Oh, honey. How long have you been married?"

"Since Saturday."

I'll never forget the concern on her face. She seemed to be mainly talking to herself when she responded, "Oh dear."

As ridiculous as this sounds, the reality is that Sad was trying to force its way back into my life. I thought for sure that God had worked it completely out, and I was naive enough to think that marriage would close the coffin on Sad once and for all.

But no, Sad was excited about tormenting me—and Bob! If Bob didn't call right away to tell me where he was, Sad would tell me I wasn't worth calling. If Bob wanted to hang out with guy friends, Sad would translate that to mean I wasn't fun enough to be with. Unbelievable this thing!

Yes, I know this is exhausting for you to read. I am exhausted just writing it. Unresolved trauma is exhausting. I had unresolved trauma, and it was not going to go away with a church service or two. Nope. This thing was deep, and it was icky. And it was stealing my REST.

I found out that my relationship with God was not just a month of recalibration to his lordship. I was going to be leaning on his love and his approval for the rest of my life.

Ten Years

Ten years. That's how long it took me to heal from the lie that I was unwanted by my husband. Only by the grace of God did Bob stick with me and build me up. I had to realize that the way I was treating Bob was connected to the unforgiveness that was in my heart.

I couldn't even tell you how many times I had to go back into the recesses of my heart and forgive people. Forgiveness, releasing the pain caused by myself and others, became the salve that finally allowed Sad to heal. I had to identify the lie that I was unwanted (that came through the trauma of my parents' divorce) and replace it with the truth from God's Word, the Bible. The Bible says that Jesus died for me because I am desperately loved (John 3:16). It also says that I was known and knit together by God in my mother's womb (Ps. 139:13). I read any Scripture passage I could on why I was wanted and loved by God. These truths began to ring true, and the lies began to break away.

Sad was finally gone. I have not viewed myself in any other light than completely loved and adored by my husband since the moment Sad was finally gone for good. I no longer see Bob's golf trips as a way for him to get away from me or the other horrible lies I used to believe. He chose me and loves me unconditionally. I finally believe that.

What anchors trauma and keeps it alive? The lies we believe. If you can uncover the lie that you have believed in your heart to be true and can replace it with what God says is true, then your mind will begin to transform. A transformed mind that believes what God says about you is a free mind—a RESTed mind.

Notice that *lie* is right in the middle of the word *believe*. Are you believing a lie that is causing unREST in an area of your life?

I don't know what your story is or what it will be. But God does. I love the stories in which people completely surrender their lives to him in a single moment, but that's not my story. I had to trip, fall, scrape, crash, and roll a few times before I realized that I was still partnering with hell, hoping to get heaven.

As painful as it feels, God will reveal to heal. He reveals the lies, then heals them with truth.

9

MAKE YOUR PEACE

To enter REST, our hearts must be at peace with God. Nearness, oneness, and peace with God are available only through accepting the sacrifice Jesus made for you and for me.

REST depends on your knowing that you are accepted and loved by God—because he himself is REST.

Have you ever felt that something is dead inside even though you are alive? You might be thinking, *Yes, but how can a person be alive and dead at the same time?*

Think about your cell phone, laptop, or any electronic device. It can be in perfect condition and dead at the same time. It needs a charge. Without a charge, it can't function.

When I take a brand-new cell phone out of the packaging, the first thing I have to do is charge it. I can refuse to charge it and try to use it. I can pick it up, pretend to dial your phone number, and begin talking into it, but that would look a lot like my toddlers pretending to talk on my old cell phones that are no longer in service. They are going through the motions, but no communication happens because the phones aren't connected to a source. A perfectly good phone can also be a dead or disconnected phone.

We can go through the motions of life and religion without being charged. We could easily attend church every Sunday, lead a Bible study, or even go to Bible college and still feel little to no connection to God. When we do "religious" things but don't sense God's presence, we are alive and dead at the same time.

From Death to Life

Jesus's objective isn't to turn bad people into good people. His objective is to bring dead people to life.

Jesus left heaven and took on human form to save you and me from eternal punishment. The Bible says that on earth he was tempted in *every* way yet did not sin (Heb. 4:15). He maintained such oneness with his Father in heaven that he didn't do or say anything that God didn't do or say. To use our phone analogy, his communication device was completely charged and connected to his Father. This is how he lived without sin and was able to move with power to heal and perform miracles.

Jesus lived purely and innocently for you and for me—not to show us up, shame us, or condemn us but to save us: "For God did not send his Son into the world to condemn the world, but to save the world through him" (John 3:17 NIV).

Before Jesus, only through the sacrifice of pure white lambs, goats, and other innocent animals could humans be purified of their sins and restored to peace with God. But even the purest spotless white lamb could not legitimately cover all the sins that had ever been committed and would be committed by human beings. Only Jesus's blood poured out would be holy enough.

God knew that we would never reach his sin-free standard. The Bible says that every person, with the exception of Jesus Christ, has fallen short of the requirements it takes to stand in the presence of a holy and perfect God (Rom. 3:23). Sin and God are like oil and water: they can't mix. Or imagine you enter a dark room and turn on a flashlight. The light overcomes the darkness. God is fully light, and darkness (sin) cannot exist in his presence. Light always dispels darkness.

Come to Life

So sin presents a problem. The Bible says that we have all fallen short of the glorious standard of God's perfect light. This means that our darkness cannot stand in the presence of God. We experience separation anxiety as a result. And when this life is over, we cannot live in a perfect heaven with a perfect God if we are polluted with darkness. Hell is where darkness lives. But God made heaven so that he could be with us. He absolutely adores us, and this is why he sent Jesus as a scapegoat to pay for our sins.

Are you getting this? God sent Jesus to stand in our place—we should have died and gone to hell for our darkness. But thank God that Jesus went to the cross, took all our sins on his body, and then went to hell for us. But he didn't stay there! He defeated Satan in hell and took back the authority that Satan had over sin. Finally, he rose from death, and the grave was found empty of his body. He defeated sin for you, for me, once and for all. He took our sins upon himself so that we could stand pure and holy in the presence of God.

When we accept what Jesus did for us, we take on a new nature and we have a new connection to the source of God. Light begins to penetrate our insides, and the darkness of sin begins to weaken, being overcome by the light. This is so important to understand because some people have made Christianity about following a list of "don't do this" and "be sure to do this." Religion isn't about what we do to get close to God. The Bible says that we can't do anything to save ourselves because we are born into sin—flawed and disconnected from God (Rom. 3:10; Titus 3:5). So we can't be good enough to earn brownie points with God. That is *not* how this works. No, we simply put our trust in the perfection of Jesus and his willingness to die in our place for our sins. Our sin bill has been paid, and we can accept full forgiveness from God. We can enter into a love relationship with God because we are no longer carrying darkness and sin. We are fully loved and able to enter fully into the light of God's presence. He says, in effect, "Come to me! Come to my throne of grace and mercy!" (Heb. 4:16). Isn't that exciting?

My friends, this is the essence of deep REST—that we are able to come fully face-to-face with God himself. Being able to stand in God's perfect light without shame or guilt is a trust like no other that brings us to a place of REST.

If you would like to acknowledge this loving and holy person of Jesus Christ right now as your Savior, reuniting you with the Father, then simply believe in your heart and confess these words aloud:

God, I realize that I have sinned against you, and I repent. Jesus, I place my trust in you as Lord of my life. I know you are able to wash me clean with your blood, which was shed for me. Thank you for taking away each sin—every one of them past, present, and future. I choose to forgive people who have hurt me, and I forgive myself for all the hurt and pain I have caused you, myself, and others. Please heal my heart in all areas where I am wounded or bruised. Turn on the light within me and dispel the darkness in my soul. I am ready to come alive in you. Show me how much you love me. Teach me who I am and how valuable I am to you. Reveal to me your secrets in the Bible. Uncover the mysteries that are written on those pages. I entrust my life to you, Lord. Here is my heart. I trust you.

Take a moment here to pause. Do not rush. Allow your heart and mind to breathe in the presence of God. You may see images or pictures of what is happening. You may feel a warmth enter your heart. Maybe light is bursting in your mind and body. Maybe you simply feel peace and stillness. This is all beautiful and perfectly fit for you. Wait patiently. Take your time. Then write what you experienced. Don't move on until you feel the nudge to keep reading.

_____

_____

_____

_____

_____

Now read aloud these two excerpts from the Bible:

Yet look at you now! Everything is new! Although you were once distant and far away from God, now you have been brought delightfully close to him through the sacred blood of Jesus—you have actually been united to Christ! (Eph. 2:13)

Even though you were once distant from him, living in the shadows of your evil thoughts and actions, he reconnected you back to himself. He released his supernatural peace to you through the sacrifice of his own body as the sin-payment on your behalf so that you would dwell in his presence. And now there is nothing between you and Father God, for he sees you as holy, flawless, and restored, if indeed you continue to advance in faith, assured of a firm foundation to grow upon. Never be shaken from the hope of the gospel you have believed in. And this is the glorious news I preach all over the world. (Col. 1:21–23)

Your heart has made peace with God. If you've encountered God in this way before, you know how powerful and life altering this is. If this is the first time you have asked Jesus to be your Savior, I want to personally congratulate you and welcome you into the family of God. There are so many secret treasures to discover from here. This isn't the end of something; this is a fresh, new beginning of something. My heart is leaping with joy for you!

The angels in heaven all rejoice when one—just one—receives God's precious gift of salvation!

10

REST REVOLUTION

I was in my early thirties. God and I had been walking together for a good while. I had two small children, my business was rolling full force, and life was active—to say the least.

With a blank piece of paper in front of me, I silently asked the Lord to speak to me. I immediately began swirling my pen around into a tornado. I will never forget the next thing I heard resound in my spirit. It would become the beginning of my REST revolution. It was an impression on my spirit, not actual words that I heard the Holy Spirit speaking. If I were to transcribe this impression into words, this is what it would say:

> Your belief system of work and REST is inaccurate: You believe, "When *this* is over, I'll be able to take a break and REST." Have you noticed that when one storm is over, another one is starting? Each storm has a center where everything is perfectly *still*. I want you to find it. I will meet you there.

"You're right, God. Life never really lets up."

I imagined myself in the center of a tornado. Debris and chaos flew all around me with violent force, but I wasn't moving. I was anchored in stillness. Then I reached out with one hand to touch the movement, and it grabbed all of me and yanked me around with unforgiving speed. This picture showed me that I could be in the storm but not a part of the storm. I could be smack dab in the center of my life, engaged and present, but not a victim of its bullying nature.

God wasn't going to remove the chaos. He was calling me into the center, into stillness.

Change Your Mind

I used to think REST and stillness were synonymous with a lack of busyness. The image of the tornado gave me a new paradigm. God was saying that I could be still and experience REST right in the middle of the chaos.

I wasn't quite sure what to do with this insight that day except that I was supposed to change my mind about REST. I sensed I was delaying REST when actually I could simply just have it.

This revelation would be the beginning of the REST revolution that led me to writing this book. God was calling me to find REST in the middle of cleaning house, raising toddlers, building a business, working on projects, and attending meetings. He was inviting me to enter these situations with full force yet without forfeiting my peace or REST. Things around me would be spinning, but I wouldn't be. I would be perfectly still.

We're Going on a Journey

For the remainder of this book, we will travel down a path that will guide you to REST. And this is a good time to remind you: the dimension of REST we are going to is a place, not an action.

In preparation for your journey, you need to identify the main thing that may be stealing your place of REST. A friend of mine said she couldn't identify with "Sad" but that "Guilt" was her bully. Guilt would speak up when God would bless her or give her opportunities. Guilt would attempt to call her out of REST and into bowing down at its offer to feel condemned.

How about you? There may be multiple lies or only a few that express themselves through emotions such as guilt, sadness, anger, sarcasm, or insecurity. Out of all the bullying emotions, which one is the most dominant for you? What would you say rattles your peace, grinds at your mind, and voices its opinion to steal your place of REST? To help you identify this, fill in the following blanks.

When I hear that someone is unhappy with me or something I've done/created, the emotion that tries to drop an anchor in me in a negative way could best be described as _____. (Example: One person may feel *unworthy* because they figure if they were good enough, people would approve of them, while another person may feel *proud* because they are certain they did nothing wrong.)

When I find out that someone has been gossiping about me, the emotion I feel the strongest is _____. (Example: One person may feel *bitter* that they've been betrayed, while another person may feel *self-pity* because this is just one more time out of many that they have been betrayed.)

When I have to confront someone to correct a situation, I am tempted to feel more _____ than I feel love for the person. (Example: One person may feel *intimidated* by the confrontation because they don't see themselves as being as powerful as the person they are confronting, while another person may feel *angry* and just bulldoze through the confrontation.)

When someone I love does something extremely generous for me, beyond what I know I deserve, the emotion that attempts to block my ability to receive that gesture of love is _____. (Example: One person may experience *guilt* and attempt to find ways to repay the person for their generosity, while another person may feel *pride* and actually reject the gift because they couldn't ever take a gift they didn't work for.)

Wounded Warrior

The frontal lobe of the brain is where we draw conclusions—it's where we rationalize our world. It takes over a quarter of a century to develop fully. This part of the brain builds conclusions based on our life experiences. For example, when I touched a hot stove, I felt pain. My brain downloaded a truth: if you touch a hot stove, you will feel pain . . . so don't touch a stove.

When we experience a traumatic event as a child (a death, a divorce, an injury, abuse, neglect, our own sin), our developing brains draw a conclusion from the event and make a "truth" out of it. In my case, a divorce resulted in the conclusion "I'm not wanted." Now, were my parents thinking this? Of course not! As an adult, I can look back and draw mature conclusions from these events, but a child's brain concludes things that seem true to them based on their limited understanding.

As an adult, I didn't deal with Sad for a long time because I came to the logical conclusion that both of my parents loved me and didn't intend to hurt me. In fact, they were wonderful people, and that trauma made no sense as an adult. So if I knew better as an adult, how is it that Sad still taunted me? How could Sad follow me into my marriage when I was completely aware that I was loved as a child?

I attempted to amputate painful events out of my life by convincing myself that I had no reason to feel pain. Logic stepped in and said, "You were loved. Get over it. It's all in your head. You're not sad. You're not lonely." Sounds easy enough. One way to understand how an adult mind can still operate with a child's perspective is by considering something called phantom limb pain. Phantom limb pain is a real condition in which a person who has had a body part amputated still feels pain in the missing limb. I still felt sadness even though the event that caused the pain was over. I'm certainly not a professional psychologist, but I can imagine that this denial of pain is a normal survival response.

Something similar happens with people who were sexually abused as children. They can have a difficult time with physical intimacy in marriage, even though the trauma took place decades earlier and the offenders and the memories have been removed—amputated—from their lives. The wounding is still attached to their insides.

Many of us are wounded warriors. We have amputated painful events and maybe even told ourselves to suck it up. Some of us may have gone to the other extreme, wearing our wounds as a badge of honor. Either way, the "intruders" we identified—guilt, sadness, bitterness, pride, and so on—are still lingering and sabotaging our REST.

Open and Closed Doors

How do the intruders we've been talking about—sadness, anger, self-pity, guilt, and so on—enter the recesses of our hearts and minds? The best way to think about this is by understanding that our soul has doors that open and shut just like any other type of door. A door is an entry point at which people or things enter and exit.

Let me explain. Here in Portland we've had a snowy winter. The kids have been going in and out of the house, playing in the snow. Every so often I feel a cold breeze rush through the kitchen, and I know immediately that one of the kids left the door open. When the door is shut, I don't feel the rush of cold air; when it's open, the air comes right in. We all know that the doors of our homes should be kept shut so that "outside" things—bugs, pests, rodents, loud noises, smells, adverse weather, and strangers—stay outside. And to take this analogy a step further, all the entry points have locks that you ultimately control.

Now, let's transition from this analogy to the house within us. Just as we live in a physical home, our mind, will, and emotions live in our soul. Let's call it our "soul home."

It is vital that we secure the doors of our soul home to prevent the invasion of ungodly emotional intruders! Ultimately, the REST we are after is a place in the soul. If ungodly and tormenting emotions are repeatedly blowing through it, we may have a door that has been left open. Whether the torment is mild or severe, our soul will never be at REST.

We must understand that ungodly emotional intruders cannot enter where there is no open door. We must be made aware, then, of how these doors are opened and how they can be shut.

When we're very young, we may experience a disappointment or a pain that can sometimes produce an underlying fear in us that this hurtful thing could happen again. If the pain is deep enough, the fear of it happening again will follow us into our adult life until it is either resolved or healed. We call this a "trauma wound," a wound that is open like the door of a home or a soul home.

A trauma can occur in a million different ways. A friend moving away abruptly without notice can be traumatic for a child, so we're not limiting trauma wounds to what we consider severe as adults. If it was severe to a child and remains an unhealed, open wound, it is considered a trauma. A child who never emotionally healed after an abrupt move of a friend, may as an adult guard themselves from deep meaningful friendships because of an underlying fear of losing a friend. This most often happens without their being aware of it.

I meet and pray with many people who have what they consider life problems. My goal is to get to the repetitive and disruptive intruder that pops up in relationships or life circumstances. Usually, I have them ask the Holy Spirit about the lie they are hearing. Here is a key: the lie will lead to the open wound.

After first verbalizing the lie they hear, I tell them to ask the Holy Spirit to show them the first time they ever heard it. It is very common for someone to say, "This is so dumb, but I'm remembering when I was eight years old . . ." and then the tears follow. Our adult brain can't comprehend why this memory is such a big deal, but the injured child in us is still hurting. As an adult, we leave that hurting child in the dust and move on with our logical life. And then we wonder why we have a sudden outburst of crying over a pile of hangers.

Jesus heals at the root, and that's the most important point I want to make right now! I want you to know that these intruders are not as random as they may feel. Often, the emotional trouble we experience today, causing unREST and anxiety, is connected to an open door, an unresolved wound, from long ago. We likely don't realize there is an open door where a lie is still functioning all these years later.

Let me share a recent example with you. Just yesterday, a friend of mine told me that when she first got married, she would get home from work and find her husband working on his computer. With excitement and kindness he would say, "Hi, honey." There was only one problem: he wouldn't look up from his computer; his eyes stayed locked on the screen. She felt anger and resentment because it made her feel as if she didn't exist.

After some time, the Lord revealed to her what was really going on. As he loves to do for us, he went after the root. He reminded her that as a little girl, when she asked her mom if she would watch a movie or play a game with her, her mom sweetly said yes but never looked up from her game of solitaire on her computer. Aha! Do you see the connection? The enemy used that lack of eye contact to tell her that she is alone and unimportant. Now, fast-forward decades later. Her husband is acknowledging her with words but not with his eyes. There is the trigger! There is an open door in her soul from a childhood wound that is causing an ungodly intruder named "rejection" to torment her. Rejection says, "See, there is all the proof you need: once again, you don't matter."

Just to make sure you get this and really understand how the enemy will use a truth to sell a lie, let me share a very silly example. Truth: a garage is designed to house a car. Lie: when I'm in the garage, I am a car. So you see? The enemy always points out something true to validate a lie. For my friend, the truth was that her husband didn't make eye contact with her, which the enemy used to attempt to validate the lie that she didn't matter to him.

How do we close the doors? These open wounds can be closed. We must surrender our will to the healing process so that we can live in the bliss of REST, a very real place. Most of the time, doors close when we forgive the person involved in the event that traumatized us. This person is oftentimes ourselves. The key to total healing is found in total forgiveness. I cannot emphasize this enough. There are volumes of books written on this subject, including the Bible! Just know this: a person could uncover every open wound, recall every traumatic event, and recognize every open door, but without forgiveness, they will remain unhealed. There is no hope for change or a place of REST if there is no forgiveness.

I know it's hard to forgive someone who has deeply wounded you. Trust me, I've been there. It can be maddening to think you have forgiven someone and then there it is again, that icky feeling in your heart when you think of them. I want to share three pieces of wisdom. First, to forgive someone doesn't mean you are reconciling the relationship. You may be forgiving someone in your heart with whom you will never speak again, or perhaps they have died. Second, during this process, you need to give yourself permission to go through the stages of grief. These godly expressions are to be honored within you. Third, the best way to dislodge a sticky hair ball of unforgiveness is to pray for the person. I mean to truly pray for them to be blessed. The more you offer prayer for them, the more the unforgiveness and pain lose their grip. One day, you'll realize you are healed because the resentment is gone and the door is closed.

Now, back to my friend. In order to close the door to the lie that she is unimportant and rejected, she had to forgive her mom in her heart. She had to repent of hanging on to the resentment and extend compassion to her. She had to forgive her mom for not being perfect and *let go of the loss.* When she did, the door that was once open to ungodly emotions was now healed and shut. In fact, repentance put a padlock on it. She no longer felt anger rise up in her soul when her husband addressed her while looking at his computer. Obviously, making eye contact with people is important and communicates love, but I'm not making a point as to whether this behavior is right or wrong. I'm highlighting the fact that an unhealed childhood pain will pop up in some way later in life, and the connection between the two can be difficult to recognize.

Do Not Fear

I want to share a story with you, but first I want to address the possibility that after reading this story you may think, *Oh no! I bet I've caused trauma to my family because of XYZ.* The truth is there isn't a single one of us who has raised our kids perfectly or been the flawless spouse, friend, or child. Everyone at some time in their lives causes other people to experience pain.

I used to carry a lot of fear that I was damaging my kids by my stupid mistakes and shortcomings. I went to the Lord with this fear in my heart that my kids would be messed up or reject me later in life. The Lord had to lovingly help me face reality in order to heal my fear. He spoke to my heart, "Yes, Jenny, you've hurt people." Whether intentionally or unintentionally, I have said and done things that caused others to feel rejected, alone, confused . . . and the list goes on. Each of my kids and my husband and most of my friends would have the opportunity to forgive me for actual hurtful things I've said and done.

I understood that though my kids may hold unforgiveness in their heart for where I fell short, they will need to lay it at the foot of the cross. There, they will have to give their pain to Jesus and learn that he is the only one who can meet their deepest need to be loved perfectly.

Now, this may sound like terrible news to you, but I suddenly felt better because God was dealing with me and teaching me truth in a way that was gentle, kind, and very matter-of-fact. He was calling me to release the idolatry in my heart of wanting to be perfect so as to avoid my fear of rejection (there's that root of fear) and to humble myself and put him alone on the altar of perfection. Then I felt him say three profound things:

- "Don't make this about you and how perfect you want to be. This is about how perfect I am. I am the perfect love your kids are looking for and need. Because you cannot fulfill this, they will come find it in me."
- "If I didn't already know you were going to blow it, I wouldn't have willingly undergone the brutality of the cross. I did it because I knew that no human could live a life without sin. You are no exception."

- "Don't parent your children from your own unresolved trauma. Rather than being afraid that you are causing your children pain, repent for holding on to the pain from your parents. If you don't release this pain to me and fully forgive them, you will always be afraid of your own parenting. Fear makes you overcompensate."

I've heard it said that all fear can be narrowed down to one or more of the following three fears:

- I'm all alone.
- I have no one to help me.
- I don't have what it takes.

The enemy uses fear. A moment of distress allows him to slip through an open door and whisper a lie. These lies are the emotional intruders we've been talking about. The devil is called the father of lies because his purpose is to lie to us. He is after our God-given identity, which is to love and be loved. If he can separate us from God's love, then he can make it almost impossible for us to receive love for ourselves and give it to others freely.

Can you see why the enemy loves to instill fear? Fear can cause so much pain that we have difficulty opening up to God and allowing a love affair to ensue between him and us. But I am living proof that if you open your heart to Jesus and trust him as the Great Physician, he will heal you with truth. The lies will fall off your identity, and the pain will fade and then finally go. For many of you, the process starts with letting go of pretending you're not hurt. For others, it may mean letting go of the idea that hurt is your identity and you don't know who you are without the wound. Forgiving yourself and others is the key to the healing process. This is not a one-time event; it is quite the opposite. Wholeness is a lifelong process, but with intentionality and a humble heart, you can walk in more and more freedom.

Jesus came to heal the sick. No matter how old or new the wound is, Jesus has truth to heal it. We all have wounds. Jesus desperately wants to heal yours if he hasn't already. Let's stop here and intentionally release people we may be holding captive in our hearts with unforgiveness. Again, this is the key to true REST. Pray this with intention in your heart:

God, you know me. You know what I've been through. You know the open doors in my heart. You know my woundings. I'm ready for total healing. I'm ready for the doors to be shut so that I can experience a still heart and mind. I am asking for your grace and protection in the process. I want REST. I want to be free from the intruder of _____ [name as many as you need to]. *Shut the door of open access. Shut all generational doors the enemy has had access to as well. Please show me where unforgiveness has blocked healing* [take your time and list all the people toward whom you hold any bitterness or hardness in your heart] *for the pain I am aware of right in this moment. I release all of them to you. Please cover me in my tears, awaken me if I go numb, comfort me if I get angry, and draw me back if I take off running. You are my REST. I REST in your largeness, in your majesty. I am your RESTed daughter. My portion is REST.*

What I have learned is that fear will arrest my REST. It will not allow me to enter the place of REST because fear is the opposite of REST. Make note of this as we travel on together.

Seven Ways—Let's Begin

I have identified seven ways for you to find full, surrendered REST. Each way leads to an experience of deeper REST and peace. As you take these steps, you will feel anxiety, stress, depression, and unREST dissipate from your heart and mind. At the same time, clarity, creativity, joy, and peace will begin to insulate you. God, after all, is REST.

PART 2

SEVEN WAYS TO REST

11

WAY 1

LEAN

*B*efore I experienced true REST, I considered REST to be something a person did: get a massage, grab a mani-pedi, or curl up on a Friday night with Netflix. In my old paradigm, RESTing was synonymous with relaxing. This is why I delayed REST. I couldn't relax, I believed, or my life would fall apart.

That day at my kitchen table as I drew the tornado, I realized the Lord was undoubtedly telling me that REST was right in the center of my everyday life. REST was a place, not a treat or a behavior. I didn't have to put off REST until a convenient time or schedule time for REST. He was REST, and he was right there.

This morning I was sitting in my favorite chair, enjoying a few silent moments before my kids woke up. I heard one of them come down the stairs and then another. Time to make breakfast. I shot up out of my chair and realized I had stood up too quickly. You know what that feels like. I got extremely dizzy and reached out for the nearest stable object, which was the cabinet that holds our television. I leaned on it until the blood could catch up to my head. If I hadn't leaned on something, I may have fallen over or hilariously stumbled into the kitchen.

REST requires leaning. If I am RESTing, I am putting my weight on something. If we still feel wobbly, we haven't reached out to a stable support. If I had reached out for one of my kids to lean on, they probably would have gone down with me because they are not as strong as I am. If you are leaning on people, drugs, alcohol, overeating, overworking, pornography, or yourself to support you in the dizzy spells life throws at you, you are probably experiencing a great deal of disappointment when they move out from underneath you or collapse to the floor with you. We've all tried leaning emotionally on people or things that ultimately have let us down. They just weren't strong enough to hold us up.

If I were to tell you that there is a stable and steady support that can hold you up under all conditions 24/7, would you want that? Some of you don't know what it feels like to have support and stabilizers underneath you. People who didn't have supportive and emotionally present parents often find themselves doubting this is possible. As children, we frame our world with our experiences, so if we didn't have someone to lean on as a child, leaning may feel very unsafe. I am sorry for that. This makes adult life difficult and stressful because we haven't had an experience that communicated to our brains that leaning is safe. We cannot see that our support is right in front of us.

Hidden in Plain Sight

A few months back I was looking for a powder vitamin drink packet in my kitchen drawer. I was rapidly scattering odds and ends back and forth in the drawer wondering where in the world the packet had gone to. I was rummaging around trying to find it, but for the life of me I could not. My assistant was there, so I asked her, "Have you seen my vitamin drink packet?"

She walked over to the drawer, put her finger on top of it in front of my face, and said with a smile, "Right there."

What in the world? Plain as day, there was the packet I was looking for. But rather than a single packet, it was an entire box of packets. There it was larger than life right in front of my eyes, for goodness' sake!

So often we don't see what is right in front of us, available in abundance, because it isn't in the form or shape we think it should be packaged. As with my drink packet, I was looking for REST in a single, little package such as a Friday night Netflix show, an afternoon power nap, a vacation, or a massage. I was looking for REST in restful activities. I was looking for such small doses of REST and relaxation that I couldn't see the largeness of God himself right in front of me.

In him is REST—not just hints and little nibbles of REST but an endless supply of permanent REST. My soul could be at REST 24/7 as I went about my everyday life. I had to make the transition from REST being an activity or a behavior to REST being a person who was right there.

> God is our refuge and strength,
> an ever-present help in trouble. (Ps. 46:1 NIV)

Who is God?	our refuge and strength
Where is God?	he's ever present; right here, right now, for always
What is he doing?	helping us
With what?	trouble

Do you believe this? Write down your thoughts here. Be honest with yourself.

_____

_____

_____

_____

_____

_____

_____

_____

_____

You may have a hard time believing this because of the trouble you've experienced. It didn't seem like anyone, including God, was helping you in your trouble. If this is the case for you, it is important that you understand that God gave you free will to choose him to lean on. You are not a puppet on his string. He gave all of us the gift of free will.

In the middle of writing that paragraph, I heard my one-year-old crying upstairs from her crib. I stopped what I was doing and went up to hold her and rock her back to sleep. She didn't fight it. She laid her head on my shoulder and immediately fell into REST. She threw one arm over my shoulder and tucked the other arm tightly under mine. She found her REST in me because she hasn't yet discovered how to find it in God, the only perfect source of REST. This is the nature and heart of

God: when we cry out in trouble, he is quick to respond and to offer his strong arms for us to lean on. Can you sense the REST in that?

Help Me Help You

If you are a parent, you know that your child can refuse your help at times. Especially as they get older, they will experiment with finding their own solution. This is an important part of development. But sometimes you get a stubborn one who refuses your help and isn't making any progress on their own. You think, *I can absolutely help you with that, but you aren't letting me.*

God probably thinks the same thing about us. He could just zap us with magic dust, but that's not God's heart. He is a person. He comes to you and me as the Holy Spirit, who is a person. He is a Father. Fathers don't zap their children and make them do things, although, now that I think of it, that could be handy (all the parents said amen). No, rather than zapping us, he extends his hand, and we have the choice as to whether we will reach out and grab it.

It takes a humble person to receive help. Are you humble?

To immerse yourself in this first way to find REST, become hyperaware of this present moment. Where are you right now? What sounds do you hear around you? What thoughts are running through your mind? Become extremely aware of your present state of mind and atmosphere.

Are you there? Okay, now I want you to soften your heart. Is it open?

Next, humble your heart.

Then, let go of control.

85

Now, ask God these questions and then patiently and peacefully wait for him to give you a response, an impression, or a visual picture in your mind. Write what you experience.

Lord, how much do you love me?

_____

_____

_____

Lord, are you here right now?

_____

_____

_____

Lord, are you my refuge and my strength?

_____

_____

_____

Lord, do you desire to be my support at all times, including times of trouble?

_____

_____

_____

If you didn't feel or see anything clearly, that's okay. Go back and try again. Sometimes it takes a minute to get our radio tuned to God's station. Be patient and compassionate with yourself. I absolutely promise you that if you draw near to God, he will draw near to you.

Why Are You So Afraid?

There is an incredible story in the New Testament about Jesus sleeping during a very stressful moment. He and his disciples are in a boat, caught up in a storm. It's dark out, and Jesus is asleep on a cushion in the stern. The waves are crashing, and the boat is filling with water. The disciples lose it. Apparently, Jesus doesn't care if they die—or so they think.

> Later that day, after it grew dark, Jesus said to his disciples, "Let's cross over to the other side of the lake." After they had sent the crowd away, they shoved off from shore with him, as he had been teaching from the boat, and there were other boats that sailed with them. Suddenly, as they were crossing the lake, a ferocious tempest arose, with violent winds and waves that were crashing into the boat until it was all but swamped. But Jesus was calmly sleeping in the stern, resting on a cushion. So they shook him awake, saying, "Teacher, don't you even care that we are all about to die!" Fully awake, he rebuked the storm and shouted to the sea, "Hush! Calm down!" All at once the wind stopped howling and the water became perfectly calm. Then he turned to his disciples and said to them, "Why are you so afraid? Haven't you learned to trust yet?" (Mark 4:35-40)

This reminds me of my sweet little Esther. For several weeks when I dropped her off at dance, she asked, "Are you going to come pick me up?" *No, I think I'll leave you here all week.* Okay, a little release of sarcasm there. I never said it out loud—but come on! After years of being 100 percent dependable to care for her, day in and day out, why would I all of a sudden forget about her? *Why are you so afraid? Haven't you learned to trust yet?*

A sudden fear came over her. This fear forced her to question my goodness, and it overrode the fact that I'd been good to her time and time again. Fear, when given a platform within us, announces its point of view. It yells, "You're all alone."

This fear comes from the perception that a caring and protecting God is nowhere in sight. When the perception of "It's all up to me" becomes a deeply rooted belief, it creates an undercurrent of anxiety. This amount of anxiety varies for different people, but none of us can truly live in REST if we don't believe we're cared for by someone greater than ourselves. As humans, we are not designed to carry this type of burden; therefore, we are unable to enter that sweet place of REST we are after. Sometimes we are like the disciples, feeling as if we have been forgotten—left for dead.

Fear Is Ridiculous . . . or Is It?

We boarded a small charter plane to fly to an African safari. Hannah, my oldest, started panicking as the flight bumped its way through the sky. She started trembling, and by the look on her face, she was on the verge of a full-blown panic attack.

I said, "Hannah, don't be ridiculous! We are not going to crash. We are completely protected by God, so you need to pull it together." I have to admit I was annoyed by her fear. She had flown so many times, and all of a sudden she was afraid? It made no sense.

To help her really grasp how ludicrous her fear was, I said, "And besides, I have promises over my life that God has given me that are unfolding many years from now, and so do you. I can promise you that we are going to live many more years." That didn't seem to help much, and she squeezed my hand so hard that it hurt.

We landed safely, as I knew we would. I knew Hannah would love the wildlife because she is an animal magnet. Dogs and cats are attracted to her, and she has a special affection for animals of all kinds. I'm not like that. I grew up with animals, but in my late teens, I had a traumatic encounter with a mad cat in the middle of the night. Yes, it was kind of like one of those pet horror shows. (No laughing.)

I asked our safari guide, "Which animal is considered the most dangerous?"

"The water buffalo," he responded. "They don't have a comfort zone. Other animals have a comfort zone, but water buffalo are always alert. For this reason, they are the most dangerous."

Note to self: *the water buffalo is deadly.*

I knew we were safe because as long as the passengers of the safari truck stay in the vehicle, the animals don't see humans as separate objects. Apparently, they just see a large object and all humans in the truck blend into the mass. But if one of us were to jump out of the truck (bad idea), the animal would recognize us as an entrée. Obviously, no one in their right mind jumps out of the truck.

It was the second day of the safari, and we had seen every animal available to see. It was incredible. Walking back to my room on the wooden planked bridge, I was enjoying the quiet sounds of nature until I saw Hannah outside of our room. "Hey, Mom! Come look!" She had her camera out and was as happy as could be. She was snapping pictures of a water buffalo standing about twenty feet in front of her. They were staring at each other. I couldn't tell if he was as fond of her as she was of him.

"Hannah!" I whisper-yelled with everything in me. "Put the camera down *right now*! Get in the room! That thing can kill us!"

She glanced over her shoulder at me and said with utter disgust, "Don't be ridiculous, Mom."

We're dead, I thought to myself. Forget every one of God's promises that I had spouted off the day before in the airplane. Those were as good as dead too.

I stood there, afraid to move. The water buffalo eventually wandered off. Hannah bounced back to the room with glee. I was tiptoeing and counting my blessings. How could we have interpreted that moment so differently?

The tables had turned. The day before, Hannah's fear of crashing had been a ridiculous and laughable "nothing" to my faith. Now Hannah was rolling her eyes at my fear.

Reflecting on the juxtaposition of those moments, I heard in my spirit, "Fear doesn't make any sense . . . until it's your own."

Are You Trusting the Fear or the Father?

The fear of dying made sense to the disciples that day in the boat. The boat was filling with water, for crying out loud! I can't say I wouldn't have responded in the exact same way.

We have to realize that fear, in and of itself, is usually all bark and no bite. In the moment, though, are we able to discern that what we are feeling is fear and not truth? Or are we treating our fear as an absolute logical fact?

A boat filling up with water surely seems like a logical reason to panic . . . until we realize that this "logic" is really just fear.

Water may be in the boat, but Jesus is too. Your finances may look like a disaster, but Jesus is in your boat. Your health may be declining, but Jesus is in your boat. Fear must be found out and trumped by greater truth.

If we think our fear makes sense, then we will lend it power. We will say, "This is a *fact*, so it must be the highest truth." In what seems like a logical conclusion, fear wins the moment. Even worse, the longer we believe in the fear, the more power it gains, eventually becoming a stronghold of the mind. A stronghold is a fortress of fear that becomes very strong and difficult to tear down.

At Universal Studios, we toured the movie sets. The buildings looked like solid brick and wood, but our guide said they were made of foam. Have you thought that maybe what you have determined to be stone or fact is really foam? Fear is fake.

The devil is committed to convincing you that your storms are going to kill you. Until you are convinced that Jesus is more real than your foam facts, you may live in a fortress of fear. You may bow to fear for the rest of your life.

There is no REST in a fortress of fear. We take our first step toward REST when we turn from our fear and lean on the Father.

> Trust in the LORD with all your heart
>   and lean not on your own understanding. (Prov. 3:5 NIV)

Learning from Jesus in the Storm

With each sentence of the story of the storm, I could see how my life could fit right into this story. Being still means we don't have to freak out during the storms. Let's look at this story and see what we can learn from it.

God Cares

We should be careful not to misinterpret God's RESTful silence as "not caring" or "leaving us for dead" as the disciples did. Jesus was sleeping; he was not panicking. There was nothing to be afraid of because he was in complete oneness with God. This father-son relationship is similar to a child being bullied on a playground. The child is scared until his dad comes, picks him up, and speaks to the bully. Fear leaves because someone bigger than the bully shows up.

We Are Funnels

My suspicion is that Jesus was intentionally getting out of the way and giving the disciples an opportunity to exercise their own faith. I believe that Jesus was giving them a chance to hush the storm with their own voices by coming into perfect alignment with Father God.

Imagine a waterfall in the heavens that allows the love and power of God to come pouring down to earth. Jesus simply aligned his spirit under this outpouring, in full light and sight of Father God. Jesus knew he was perfectly loved and adored, so he felt unashamed standing under the flow of the full power and love of God. The acceptance and affirmation of his Father made him able to REST.

Take a moment to activate this in your own spirit. Imagine now that your spirit, full of faith, steps into the throne room of God. His love and power draw you in, and the love you feel flows in you and right out of you. Spend a moment to see this divine alignment and flow of his love and power. This is your RESTing place.

You and I are called to stand under the lavishing love of Almighty God. Our Father, your Father, wants you to stand fully in the light of his power and love. He wants you to have faith—not in yourself but in his love and acceptance of you. If you've received Jesus Christ as your personal Savior, then God sees you as pure and righteous in his sight. You don't have to glance away when he looks at you. You can look back with full assurance of his love and approval of you. Your acts, good or bad, are not what he's measuring you by. You are measured by what Jesus Christ did for you. Have you put your faith in Christ? If so, you are invited to be a funnel and outsource his power and love to the people around you and the circumstances that you encounter in life.

We Are Called to Live Our Faith Out Loud

Three of us were on a ski lift several years ago. We were headed to the top of the mountain when, halfway up the hill, the lift stopped. Normally, it restarts quickly, but in this instance, it stalled for what felt like way too long. The wind began to pick up, and we swayed from side to side. The wind cut through us, and it was frigid, to say the least. Realizing that the lift wasn't moving and we were stuck, my friend, her son, and I started to pray. We began rebuking the wind and telling it to "Hush!"

Some may think it was presumptuous or arrogant of us to think that we could stop the wind, but the Bible says to apply our faith in God. The story of the disciples in the storm prompted us to live our faith out loud and to let it come from our voices. After all, Jesus didn't *think* the storm away. He rebuked it with his voice.

We prayed, and the wind stopped. A white winter calm came over us—so much peace. Then the lift motor kicked in, and up the hill we went.

This was a moment when we could have panicked and asked God if he even cared. But it was also an opportunity to align ourselves with Father God and allow his power to funnel through our faith and our voices. We were surely thinking, *Stop!* Most of the people on the lift were probably thinking the same thing. The difference was our voices. This is a small example, but I tell it to show you how you can begin to practice using your faith to funnel the power and love of God to earth, especially through your voice.

I am still learning to use my voice to funnel God's power and love.

I recently got shingles, which was really miserable. I was praying and leaning. Waiting. Waiting. Waiting for healing. Then four days after the outbreak, once I realized this thing was really happening, I got a prescription. Some people believe that perfect faith translates into not using medication. But I heard a pastor once say that if a burglar breaks in, you grab the alarm clock, the chair, the lamp—all of it—and chuck them at the intruder. I love when God heals instantly through prayer alone, which I have witnessed countless times, but my experience is that he has also given us other solutions to win the battle. Medicine, nutrition, and wellness therapies are all remedies in your arsenal. But your voice holds the most power of all.

The shingles virus certainly doesn't exist in heaven, so this became my permission to tell it to "Hush!" I held a large blue pill in my hand and heard the Holy Spirit prompt me to speak to the virus. Remembering what David said to Goliath right before flinging a stone at the big giant and killing him, I said, "You might come at me with a virus, but I'm coming at you with the power of God. Who are you to come against the living

God?" I threw that big blue pill back in my throat as if I was flinging a stone at a giant.

You see, the shingles virus wasn't coming against little me all by myself. The shingles virus was coming against the living God who lives in me through the Holy Spirit. In the presence of God, it could not stand. No giant can stand in the presence of God.

I called a few faithful prayer friends and asked them to pray for me. Do you have a few friends who will pray for you when the storms hit? You must have some friends who are willing to live their faith out loud.

We REST on the Cushion of His Goodness

The fact that Jesus was lying on a cushion really catches my attention. Not one word in the Bible is random or irrelevant. Asking the Holy Spirit about this, I immediately discerned that this cushion is a very important model for us. This RESTing place is not a hard wooden boat. To me, the softness of the cushion describes something about the goodness of God.

We REST on the cushion of his goodness. The awareness that he is good allows us to REST and be comforted no matter what is happening. If he is good, then we can relax and stay light in heart and mind. We are not RESTing on a hard surface—no! We are RESTing on the assurance that in any situation, God is good and he is in control. How can we truly enter REST if we don't believe that God is always good despite the storm?

It's Darker during a Transition

This story of Jesus and his disciples highlights a time of transition. Jesus said, "Let's cross over to the other side" as an announcement of transition.

Are you going to the "other side" of a place in life right now? Maybe it's an actual move, or maybe it's a new baby, a new marriage, or the loss of a loved one. Maybe it's a career change or a change in your belief system. Life is full of transitions.

Notice that in the story, it grew darker during the transition. Darkness during a transition can simply be all of the unknowns that come with the change. Even a positive transition, like adding a baby to the family, comes with new questions that may not have answers. During a transition, we don't see as well because the pathway before us isn't as clear and we can dream up a hundred different possible outcomes. Our life looks scarier in the dark than it does in the light. But the fantastic news is that Jesus, although hidden in the dark, is still there. He didn't leave the disciples in the darkness of transition, and he won't leave you.

We Need to Power Up in a Crowd of Two

Jesus and the disciples left the crowd behind. A crowd can be uplifting and provide strength. I love a powerful church service, and I'm the first to want to go to any type of conference where there is power and energy. But after the concert, after the church camp, after the church service, the crowd goes away. Sometimes that's when the storms come. Things that weren't scary in a crowd become frightening without the power of numbers. But let's not forget that even if the crowd is gone, Jesus is still there. It's easy to get our strength from a crowd rather than from Jesus. We must learn to tap into a power that is not our own and not found in others. This is the power of the Holy Spirit. You and Jesus are all you need to hush a storm.

We're Not the Only Ones Weathering a Storm

Other boats sailed with them. In the middle of our storms and chaos, we may be tempted to think that we are the only ones experiencing a storm. The disciples were not the only ones in the storm. Be careful that "victim" doesn't become your identity. We all encounter storms.

God Is in Your Boat

God is not hiding from you. It may be dark, and it may be difficult to see him. However, he's not sleeping or apathetically laying in your boat. He is calling you to lean into the Father, lean into the payment Jesus made at the cross, and come fully under the flow of his power and love. He is working day and night to call you to him and into divine alignment. Can you believe that through Jesus Christ you are fully loved and not measured by your merits or mistakes?

Because we tend to be "I'll believe it when I see it" type of people, we can get frustrated if God appears to be sleeping or invisible. The Greek word for *Holy Spirit* is *pneuma*, which is "to breathe, blow, primarily denotes the wind."[1] I think this describes God well. As with the wind, we can't see God, but we can feel him and see what he moves and touches. When the trees sway, we know that a wind is moving and touching them. The wind can be felt and what it touches can be seen—and the same is true with God.

Just as I had held and comforted my baby girl when she was crying, God is waiting for you to call on him so he can do the same. And then you lean into his arms. You REST your head on his shoulder. You REST on the cushion of his goodness. Your soul relaxes, and you REST under the flow of the Father's love and power.

To practice this first way of finding REST, envision yourself leaning on God and aligning with him this week. Practice the art of leaning on him all day and all night. Wake up leaning. Go to bed leaning. Go about your day leaning. During happy moments, lean. During challenging moments, lean. And by all means, use your voice over every fear this week. Command fear to hush. Don't think it away—get under the funnel and tell the fears to hush.

God is REST, and he is right here.

12

WAY 2

LET GO

Several years ago, Bob and I went to a Hillsong Church conference in Los Angeles. Pastor Brian Houston, the lead pastor, preached a message centered around the meaning of a song that was written and produced by their church, "Oceans (Where Feet May Fail)." The lyrics of the song convinced me to leave the safety of the boat and step out onto the water, where sinking is a real possibility.

At the time, I was thirty-eight years old with three kids over the age of six. We had just come up for air. No more diapers, sippy cups, and toddler tantrums. And then a strange thing happened: I felt that God was calling us to have another baby. This was a huge stretch for both of us, especially for Bob, to think we would "start over." It was a risky idea that confronted our comfort and perceived control. Bob and I had extremely heated fellowship over the matter of what would happen to our lives if we were to add more moving parts. Simply put, we were afraid of not being in control. Bob was convinced that we couldn't handle another child, and frankly, he was right. But perhaps that was the point.

When we heard Pastor Brian talk about the great adventure we are called to live, we realized that we had unconsciously backed away from risk and adventure. Early in our marriage, we had embraced risk and adventure because we didn't have much to lose. Approaching the edge of the cliff had become a bit more challenging, though, because we perceived we had more at stake. Out of a desire to protect our emotions and keep chaos at a minimum, we had taken tiny steps away from the edge.

God was calling us back to an adventurous, unpredictable, most likely messy life. We talked over dinner and realized that we had been the happiest when we were standing with our toes hanging over the edge of life. It was time to be adventurous and step out of the boat—outside of the box—and walk on water.

In the labor room, Bob had tears rolling down his face as my contractions increased. Eden Deborah Donnelly entered the world, and I can tell you that Bob has not been the same since. One look at her, and he was changed right there in that hospital room. Control and predictability fell off of him. A fear of losing control didn't have a grip on him anymore because he decided that losing control would be exactly what he would do. The decision to allow another Donnelly into our lives was one of the greatest decisions we've ever made. She is a gift to our family, and neither of us can imagine life without her.

The kind of adventure I'm referring to is a lifestyle, not a moment.

Surprisingly, the day I came home from the hospital, I laid Eden on the changing table and a thought hit me from out of left field. My heart swelled with a knowing: "We're going to have another one." I thought Bob would say, "No way! This is far enough out of the boat." But he didn't. He said, "Why not?" He was so free that it caught me off guard. He had been delivered of the façade that he could control his life. He let go of control and stepped into the adventure. This adventurous life was way more fun than being a control freak.

Nineteen months later, Mercy Evangeline was born. We have five kids, and we are crazy on purpose. The adventure is a thrill and, ironically, more RESTful!

A Great Paradox

The more we try to control our lives, the more we lose our REST.

Bob wanted two kids, because that's what he thought he could control. And now, he has five. We are way in over our heads, and it's an adventure, baby! Bob's life paradigm on this issue so dramatically changed that he now shares his testimony with audiences nationwide. Control is an illusion—life is meant to be a great adventure. If you knew how much Bob loved predictability and control, you would know what a changed man he is. The proof is in the pudding. He is beaming with more joy, surrender, and REST than ever before. He is truly free from the clutches of the control monster.

How about you? Do you find yourself trying to control chaos so you don't feel out of control? Again, we're going for total honesty here. In what areas is it easy for you to give up control, and in what areas is it more difficult?

_____

_____

_____

_____

_____

How is it that the more we try to control things, the less peace we have? The problem with trying to control everything is that we become the god of our own lives. We try to control what isn't controllable—that's why control is an illusion, a façade. There are thousands of variables we cannot control. Don't be deceived! We attempt to control our circumstances when we need our outer lives to satisfy our inner lives. But if we are leaning on God, we can let go of the things that are truly not in our power to change.

Can you control how your kids behave? Sure, you can lead them into wonderful character (and please do), but you can't control their hearts. They are their own persons. We discover this as they become toddlers and teens.

Can you control how your coworkers treat you?

Can you control the weather?

Can you control interruptions that happen several times a day?

Can you control traffic?

Can you control how your spouse treats you? Treating your spouse with love and respect will definitely pay off. But can you control your spouse? If you have been married for any length of time, you know the answer is a laughable no. Then why are you trying to?

Although we've discussed how we can partner our faith with God, like telling the wind to "hush," God is sovereign. Ultimately, only God has access to the heart. Only God controls the weather. Only God knows why traffic is heavy when you are running late. God is also in control of the interruptions. This is one of the tensions we live in as Christians—we exercise our faith and at the same time let go of control.

God is God. He is absolutely in control, holding the entire world, ecosystem, and universe together. In fact, you weren't in control of whether you woke up this morning with a heart beating and breath in your lungs. You don't even know how long you will live. God was the One who decided to put his breath in your lungs so you could live another day. Do you see how ridiculous it is to approach our lives with the egotistical idea that we can control things? What a waste of energy.

Control is entirely different from leadership and responsibility. Bob and I have taught leadership for many years. Leadership is influence. You are wise to be a godly influence for your spouse and your children. You are wise to influence your coworkers in a positive way. You are wise to influence your neighbors with love and energy. But control their responses and behavior? Hah! Never going to happen. You do the influencing in a positive way, and then you let go and let God take care of the outcome. I'm telling you—this is freedom. This is REST!

Orphans No More

When we clutch our lives, relationships, and projects with a white-knuckled grip, we don't realize that we've scooted the God of all creation into the passenger seat. Maybe he's in the backseat. Or worse, maybe he's not allowed in the car. As control freak drivers, we risk stepping into an orphan spirit. An orphan is someone who doesn't have any parents, no one to care for them. How sad.

If we are living as orphans, we have difficulty taking a deep breath and relaxing in the midst of chaos because we think it's up to us to manage, fix, and tidy things back to their place. Some of you don't realize yet that God wants to help you and bless you. He is a Father—the best parent. He wants to drive your car and let you be his copilot.

Along the way, he pulls the car over and makes a stop. He asks you to open the door and step into a new assignment. He asks you to bring your gifts to this new job and not to fear what you do not know. He says, "I'm coming with you. If you ask me, I'll guide you." Or maybe he makes a stop and says, "It's time to change the way you think about your teenager. I'm going to show you how to help them succeed, but you're going to have to change some things about yourself for this to work." Yes, God loves to stretch us so that he can give us more. God is all about parenting us. He moves and prompts us only into the direction of good.

Jesus didn't come to take. He came to give!

A thief has only one thing in mind—he wants to steal, slaughter, and destroy. But I have come to give you everything in abundance, more than you expect—life in its fullness until you overflow! (John 10:10)

No matter what, don't worry. God is in the driver's seat now. If you took a wrong exit, he can reroute you to where you belong.

Be Still

He says, "Be still, and know that I am God;
    I will be exalted among the nations,
    I will be exalted in the earth." (Ps. 46:10 NIV)

This is one of my favorite verses in the Bible because it tells me what to do. Sometimes it just helps to have instruction, right? The Ancient Roots Translinear Bible (ARTB) helps us understand the meaning of this verse. Rather than "be still" it reads "let go," because being still is not about holding still but about letting go of your life into the entrustment of God. Now look at what comes next in the NIV translation: "and know that I am God." The ARTB states it this way: "in order to know God." In other words, "let go in order to know God." This tells me that in order to know God intimately, I need to let go of my life to see who he really is.

The Passion Translation states it this way:

> Surrender your anxiety!
> Be silent and stop your striving and you will see that I am God.
> I am the God above all the nations,
> and I will be exalted throughout the whole earth.

I love this! The Bible clearly says that in order for us to know God, we have to let go.

Last week our family went to the pool. My three-year-old was standing on the edge of the swimming pool, and I was reaching up my arms and smiling at her. "Jump to Mama!" I said. She looked apprehensive. She paused. She knew I'd been reliable up to this point, but she also knew that if I didn't catch her, she would sink. She wanted to jump, but she was torn between the thrill of adventure and potential danger. I could see her wheels turning. *Do I jump or don't I?*

This whole thing came down to me, her mom. Could I be trusted? She couldn't answer that question any other way than experientially. She had to jump to find out if I was as good as she thought I was. She couldn't know my goodness without putting herself in a situation in which I had to come through for her.

That's what the above Scripture passage means, and that's why this book is titled *Still*. Being still isn't about *holding still* on the edge of the pool where you perceive you can control your own safety. No, stillness is in your soul where everything remains calm even as God calls you to jump.

REST is found in letting go, jumping off the edge of the pool, and finding out that God will catch you. That's how you come to know God. Not by taking a religion class. Not by getting a degree in theology. It is by putting yourself in a situation in which his love is tested. This is how you come to trust his character.

Do you have a dream or a desire to do something so adventurous that it ignites your spirit just thinking about it? Perhaps you've let the fear of sinking (anxiety) freeze you on the edge of the pool and prevent you from diving into that adventure. Take some time to write down your dream here. Tell God your dream and what fears are holding you back.

_____

_____

_____

_____

_____

_____

Now pause and ask him, "In this particular dream, are you calling me to jump?"

It's important that you listen and seek wise counsel—people who know God, know you, want you to succeed, and have proven results in their lives. Broke Uncle Harry wouldn't make the wise counsel list regarding a money matter because he doesn't have any money. If you need to let go in an area of parenting, be sure to seek wise counsel from someone who has fruit to show that their parenting is successful.

If the answer is "No, you shouldn't move in that direction," then ask, "What should I be doing right now? How can I align myself with the plan you have for me?"

If the answer is yes, ask him, "Will you help me believe you will be there to catch me?" Stop and listen to what you hear the Spirit say.

Patiently wait to let God speak or give you a picture in your mind. Write down what you see or hear.

_____

_____

_____

_____

_____

To practice this second way of finding REST, envision yourself stepping behind God and allowing him to control your steps. All that stuff you can't control but really care about? Throw it into the pool and see him catch it and sort it out for you. Ask him to guide you.

See your life as an adventure—let go!

13

WAY 3

CULTIVATE INTIMACY

As a kid, you probably played the trust fall game in which you faced away from a person and fell backward—and it was up to your friend to catch you. The game was fun (if they caught you) and certainly adventurous. Now, what if a perfect stranger walked up to you and said, "Turn around and fall and I will catch you." You'd be like, "Uh, no thank you."

Why? Well, you don't know this person, so therefore you can't be sure they will catch you. The adventure is not worth the risk.

We've talked about the first two steps to REST: leaning and letting go. We can go through these motions, but over time, they're unsustainable if they're not fully supported by the right belief system. You see, our actions come from our deepest held beliefs.

For instance, if I believe that exercise is a great way to nurture myself and is important for my overall health and well-being, I will probably exercise throughout the year. If I don't really believe that exercise is important for my health, I may do it only when I am trying to lose a few pounds. I won't continue to exercise because I don't have a belief system that supports consistency. In the same way, we can practice leaning and letting go for a stretch of time, but we will make these activities a lifestyle only if we deeply believe that God is good and can be trusted.

Do leaning on God and letting go feel as if you are falling into the arms of a good friend? Or do they feel more like you are falling into the arms of a stranger or a twice-removed cousin you met one time at a family reunion? If God feels more like a distant cousin, that's a starting point. But to sustain a lifestyle of REST, you need to scoot him into a space in your heart where you call him friend. He must make his way from stranger in your mind to best friend and Almighty King. You can live in REST for the rest of your life only if you experience a friendship with him, and this can happen only by cultivating intimacy. As with any developing relationship, it takes hours and months of positive exchanges of goodness to trust that God really has your best interest in mind.

Trust

I saw a commercial the other day for a new reality show in which the bride and groom meet each other for the first time at the altar. She walks down the aisle to the groom and says, "Nice to meet you." A few minutes later, they are married. I don't know about you, but my reaction was, "You have got to be kidding me! This is an absurd idea!"

If I didn't know God, I would have a hard time saying, "I do." I couldn't make him Lord if I didn't know what he was all about. Jesus said in so many words, "If you've seen me, you've seen the Father" (see John 14:9). So if we want to know God, one of the best ways is to come to know Jesus by reading the first four books of the New Testament called the Gospels. The Gospels are eyewitness accounts of Jesus's life written by four men who walked with Jesus almost every day: Matthew, Mark, Luke, and John. *Gospel* means "good news." Jesus is good news!

Jesus was a tremendous teacher. He taught his followers how to connect with God. His teachings shed light on who he is and who God is. Remember, the goal of knowing him is trusting him—and trust produces REST.

Love Revealed

When I first asked Jesus into my heart, I understood that God loved me and had redeemed me from my shame and guilt. What I didn't yet understand was the depth to which God loved me.

"I don't think I understand how much you love me." I remember exactly where I was standing when I stopped and admitted this to God. I stood at the top of my staircase and experienced an epiphany. "I don't think I really get it." I had been a Christian for years, had experienced a tangible love from his presence in ways that had moved me to tears. He had been personally directing me and was real and relevant to my everyday life. But this sudden thought that he was *in love* with me kind of perplexed and overwhelmed me at the same time. I realized I was only ankle deep in this idea that he loved me, all of me. And not just humankind as a whole but me, Jenny.

Up until that moment, I was able to rely on my accomplishments as evidence to myself that God loved me. I obeyed him and he blessed me. But that day on the staircase, he messed me up. It was like he was erasing everything, all my accomplishments, my résumé, and my mistakes and saying, "I just love you, Jenny." He took away all I had done, and the only thing left was me—just a person with no reason why she should be loved.

I mean, I know I have a few great attributes, but I'm also no different from the next person. Yet he pulled me out of a generic view of "God loves all people" and invited me into a new view of his love: "God loves Jenny . . . not because of what Jenny has done but because of who Jenny is."

And that was the problem. I didn't know who Jenny was. I didn't really know myself apart from "doing." I was more in touch with what I could produce than with who I was without accomplishments. I told God, "You're going to have to show me. I want to understand."

Boy, say that prayer and God is off to the races. A trusted friend called me within forty-eight hours and said, "Hey, God spoke to me and said he was going to teach you all about his love." You don't say!

The next thing he told me was that he was going to change my prayer life. I was doing what I thought I was supposed to do: bring God my issues and ask him to solve them. This, in itself, was not wrong. But he revealed to me that if I went on a date with Bob and pulled out my honey-do list as my only objective in the relationship, then I defined and limited the relationship. Bob was my life manager; Bob was my fix-it guy—not my friend or companion.

Is it wrong to give your spouse a honey-do list? Of course not. But if that is the foundation of the relationship, it is going to be shallow, selfish, and de-energizing. The foundation of a healthy marriage is friendship—a loyal affection for the other person. The same is true in our relationship with God. To experience a deep and meaningful relationship with him, we must intentionally place our adoration on him for who he is, apart from the wonderful things he does for us or what we want him to do for us. If I have God, I have everything I need.

A New Way to Pray

God flipped my prayer paradigm on its head. He gave me the simple instructions to put on my favorite worship music, lie down for thirty minutes, and—this next part messed me up in the best way—do nothing. He simply wanted me to receive. This was like turning my shirt inside out because I was under the horrific assumption that it was my job to do something to keep our relationship intact. Surely I needed to do something to earn God's attention.

For the next several weeks, I lay there and listened to God's heart for me. I let myself off the performance hook. During that time, God told me things about me that made me blush. He romanced me, honestly. Some people may feel weird about that, but he just wanted to sit across the dinner table and tell me what made me special. He told me that he enjoyed me and really liked being with me. He listed the attributes that made me "me," unique and wonderful to him.

I didn't really know my value until I stopped and allowed him to do the pursuing. But I certainly didn't play hard to get. I allowed myself to become humble enough to receive affection and words of affirmation from him. I needed to be built up more than I realized.

A religiosity fell off me, and the Christian life became about a person who was in love with me. I soon found myself telling him how much I loved him too. My "God-do" list made it into our conversations, but much of the longing I had in my heart was taken care of because I allowed being filled up by his love for me to be my first priority. Can you see how important it is that you know that God loves you? Your accurate perception of what he thinks about you is vital to your REST. How can we be sure that he loves us unconditionally? The Bible states it multiple times.

Detangled

My little Eden has bouncy curls that turn into a matted mess after a few days. She absolutely hates getting her hair washed because it means I have to run a comb through the nest of knots. No matter how much detangler spray I use and how slowly I comb, we've never gotten through the process without a few tears.

We can also have knots and tangles on the inside. Anxiety causes our insides to twist, and we can sense unease, unREST, on the inside. If things are left this way too long, we can fall into depression. And if they are left even longer, we can find ourselves overtaken by a black hole. This is where we completely lose sight of the purpose for living. Scary.

Just as I sit with Eden to comb out her tangles, God desires to do the same for us. This is an intimate process. We must spend time in his arms for him to work through each knotted piece. And often we shed many tears as the knots are undone. Like Eden, we would rather avoid the pain and tears that come with the detangling process.

Dreadlocked

Look what David declared to God in Psalm 139:15–16:

> You withheld none of my bones making me in hiding,
> and embroidering me in the bottom land. Your eyes see
> my knots! (ARTB)

This totally melts my heart when I read it. This is intimacy! God put you and me together with intention and precision. Not only does God love Jenny, but he also knows Jenny's knots. And because he loves me, he wants to untangle my snags in exchange for peace.

Tangled knots, left undone, produce dreadlocks. Now, dreadlocked hair is simply a fashion choice. But when we get dreadlocked on the inside? That's dangerous. Knots, left alone, cause dread. We dread getting up in the morning. We dread simple, everyday tasks. We dread living.

I got in the shower one day and felt uneasy on the inside. I said, "Something is wrong. What's wrong with me?" I was waiting for some type of explanation for why I was feeling knotted up, but God's response was something different. "You just need a hug." I began to sob. My Daddy knew I needed love—not just from a person but from a Shepherd.

The Good Shepherd

Jesus refers to himself as the Good Shepherd who cares for and protects the sheep (us). He is the way into the sheep pen (he's the gate—our access into the pen), where we are cared for and protected by God.

Jesus knew that counterfeit shepherds would try to climb the fence of the sheep pen in order to harm us, steal from us, and destroy us. He was referring to false gods, false religion, and Satan when he spoke about thieves. Jesus said these powerful words:

> I am the Gateway. To enter through me is to experience life, freedom, and satisfaction. A thief has only one thing in mind—he wants to steal, slaughter, and destroy. But I have come to give you everything in abundance, more than you expect—life in its fullness until you overflow! (John 10:9–10)

In the sheep pen, we are at REST: fed, protected, nurtured, and blessed to overflowing. This is about as far from anxiety and depression as we can get. Under the care of our Shepherd, we can relax. It is well with our soul.

But every so often our souls become downcast and we find ourselves tangled and toppled over.

> Why, my soul, are you downcast?
> Why so disturbed within me?
> Put your hope in God,
> for I will yet praise him,
> my Savior and my God. (Ps. 43:5 NIV)

I've been told that being "cast down" is a term used for sheep that have fallen and can't get back up. They are stuck on their backs, flailing their legs in the air. After a few hours, gas begins to build up and their intestines knot up, causing pressure on their lungs. Left alone, the sheep will eventually suffocate.

When a shepherd restores a cast down sheep, he massages its legs to restore blood flow, comforts the sheep, gently turns the sheep right side up, lifts up the sheep, and holds it in a position so its knotted intestines can unwind.

What a beautiful image of what our God wants to do for us. This process of being massaged, being held, and RESTing for an extended time in the Shepherd's arms is a picture of intimacy. This is our RESTing place. When we are on our backs, stuck in knots of depression, anxiety, anger, grief, sadness, stress, or purposelessness, we have a Shepherd who wants to help.

May we yield to his love and resist the lie that he wouldn't want to hold us in our pathetic state. He calls himself the Good Shepherd because he longs to be our hero, our massager, our holder.

Known

Regardless of how well we know him, God knows us completely.

Psalm 139, written by King David, is profound. We can take every word as truth because every word of the Bible is true and inspired by God.

> Lord, you know everything there is to know about me.
> You perceive every movement of my heart and soul,
> and you understand my every thought before it even
>   enters my mind.
> You are so intimately aware of me, Lord.
> You read my heart like an open book
> and you know all the words I'm about to speak
> before I even start a sentence!

You know every step I will take before my journey even
    begins.
You've gone into my future to prepare the way,
and in kindness you follow behind me
to spare me from the harm of my past.
With your hand of love upon my life,
you impart a blessing to me.
This is just too wonderful, deep, and incomprehensible!
Your understanding of me brings me wonder and
    strength.
Where could I go from your Spirit?
Where could I run and hide from your face?
If I go up to heaven, you're there!
If I go down to the realm of the dead, you're there too!
If I fly with wings into the shining dawn, you're there!
If I fly into the radiant sunset, you're there waiting!
Wherever I go, your hand will guide me;
your strength will empower me.
It's impossible to disappear from you
or to ask the darkness to hide me,
for your presence is everywhere, bringing light into my
    night.
There is no such thing as darkness with you.
The night, to you, is as bright as the day;
there's no difference between the two.
You formed my innermost being, shaping my delicate
    inside
and my intricate outside,
and wove them all together in my mother's womb.
I thank you, God, for making me so mysteriously
    complex!
Everything you do is marvelously breathtaking.
It simply amazes me to think about it!

How thoroughly you know me, Lord!
You even formed every bone in my body
when you created me in the secret place,
carefully, skillfully shaping me from nothing to
    something.
You saw who you created me to be before I became me!
Before I'd ever seen the light of day,
the number of days you planned for me
were already recorded in your book.
Every single moment you are thinking of me!
How precious and wonderful to consider
that you cherish me constantly in your every thought!
O God, your desires toward me are more
than the grains of sand on every shore!
When I awake each morning, you're still with me.
O God, come and slay these bloodthirsty, murderous
    men!
For I cry out, "Depart from me, you wicked ones!"
See how they blaspheme your sacred name
and lift up themselves against you, but all in vain!
Lord, can't you see how I despise those who despise
    you?
For I grieve when I see them rise up against you.
I have nothing but complete hatred and disgust for
    them.
Your enemies shall be my enemies!
God, I invite your searching gaze into my heart.
Examine me through and through;
find out everything that may be hidden within me.
Put me to the test and sift through all my anxious cares.
See if there is any path of pain I'm walking on,
and lead me back to your glorious, everlasting ways—
the path that brings me back to you.

When you read this passage, how did it make you feel about the character and nature of God?

_____

_____

_____

_____

_____

Could you fall into the arms of someone like this? Could you allow God to massage you, hold you, and love you in your downcast moments?

_____

God knows you. What things would you be willing to do to get to know him so that you can make him your friend? Circle all the ones you will truly do. Hopefully, you will want to do all of them. But if this is new for you, pick one or two to begin.

- Pray (spend time with God in conversation with him and converse with him throughout the day).
- Read your Bible and seek God's love and wisdom for you.
- Journal your thoughts, desires, and disappointments so that you and God can work through them together.
- Worship (spend time praising and giving adoration to Jesus).
- Attend a Jesus-centered church.

- Connect with people who share this same journey in God.
- Fast (deny your body food for a certain amount of time to purge the selfish part of you and fill up with God).

Vulnerable

You may be asking, "When I pray, what do I say?"

The Psalms offer examples of what prayers within an intimate relationship with Christ sound like. Intimacy can be expressed this way: in-to-me-see. The author of most of the Psalms, David, trusted God so fully that he just straight-up opened his spiritual chest cavity and gave God all that was in there. He knew God could handle his fears, bad attitudes, and discouragement. Sometimes David ran to God in fear and ended a psalm in praise. Other times he expressed his joy and love for life. Still other times he pleaded with God to rescue him from his enemies.

Here is one of David's psalms in which he went to God with a transparent heart and then ended in praise and honor.

> I'm hurting, Lord—will you forget me forever?
> How much longer, Lord?
> Will you look the other way when I'm in need?
> How much longer must I cling to this constant grief?
> I've endured this shaking of my soul.
> So how much longer will my enemy have the upper
> hand?
> It's been long enough!
> Take a good look at me, God, and answer me!
> Breathe your life into my spirit.

Bring light to my eyes in this pitch-black darkness
or I will sleep the sleep of death.
Don't let my enemy proclaim, "I've prevailed over him."
For all my adversaries will celebrate when I fall.
Lord, I have always trusted in your kindness, so answer
    me.
I will yet celebrate with passion and joy
when your salvation lifts me up.
I will sing my song of joy to you, the Most High,
for in all of this you have strengthened my soul.
My enemies say that I have no Savior,
but I know that I have one in you! (Ps. 13)

I wrote a psalm a few months ago. Several hundred women were gathering for a conference called "Her Voice," and the Lord asked me to dance at it—not for people but for him. Dance is a form of worship. As a young girl, I danced, and when I danced, the pain would go away. But I had abandoned dancing many years ago. When I stopped, I didn't realize I would lose something precious. Here I was, over twenty years later, and God was asking me to dance again. I agreed because I've come to trust that whenever God asks me to do something, it is always good because he is good.

However, I was unbelievably scared to dance for many reasons, but mainly I was afraid of exposing myself. Here is the psalm I wrote in my journal as I wrestled with my fears.

Covered

I'm saying "naked" and you're saying "covered."
I am surrounded by your dignity and righteousness.
Love absorbs my nakedness.

Dancing in public is my absolute most scariest
   nightmare EVER.
Why does it feel so very vulnerable, Lord?
When I dance, I am opening all of me.
I don't like the idea of all eyes on me.
Why? Ugh.
Here we are again in this same conversation.
Help.
Dancing communicates my feelings.
I've gotten very good at not showing my feelings or
   even allowing them to be seen by me.
What are you afraid of . . . when you show emotion,
   especially through dance?
I'm afraid I'll feel weak and lame—
and the story behind my dance is one that doesn't seem
   worthy of emotion.
And yet, I am covered in your clothing of peace and
   love.
This dance will be beautiful and healing.

I danced that day, and it was healing for me and many. But first I had to work out my fears in a psalm to God. In-to-me-see. God wants to work out this life, moment to moment and prayer to prayer, with each of us.

It's your turn to write a psalm. Picture yourself crawling into a kangaroo pouch (I call it the pocket) and snuggling into the heart of your Father. How do you feel right now? With a transparent heart, write what is going on in your life and within you. Stretch your limits by going all in—spill your heart to God. End your psalm with genuine thanksgiving, praise, or whatever affection and honor you want to give him. Don't skip this! This is powerful and develops intimacy!

_____

_____

_____

_____

_____

_____

_____

_____

_____

_____

_____

_____

To practice this third way of finding REST, I want you to cultivate intimacy with God this week. Walk with him as your best friend. Allow him to quench your emotional thirst. We've all been thirsty before and grabbed a soda or juice only to realize that our thirst wasn't quenched. We can accidentally develop intimacy with things and people when we are thirsty to know and be known. This week, rather than reaching for those things that don't ultimately satisfy or bring you REST, reach for God through one of the activities you committed to in this chapter. These things will quench the thirsty place inside you that is longing for intimacy.

This thirsty place can be satisfied only by the One who is love—Jesus, the Lover of your soul.

14

WAY 4

PUT ON PRAISE

*B*efore we discuss the fourth way to find REST, I want you to take a simple assessment. We'll refer to it later in the chapter.

How do you feel emotionally *right this second*? Write your honest answer. (Examples: bored, tired, happy, focused, lost, intimidated, light, heavy, sad, regretful, anxious, stressed, passionate, expectant, blah, safe, unsafe, etc.) You are *not* declaring that this is who you are. It could (and probably will) change in the next five minutes. This isn't a label or a declaration. You are simply allowing yourself to voice an emotion. There is no evaluation in this. The only right answer is your honest one.

Right this second, I am feeling _____

_____.

Did you answer honestly? Great! Now let's look at how to dress for REST.

A Beautiful Outfit Can Uplift a Heart

My nine-year-old, Esther, loves to go into my closet and put on my dresses. She doesn't care that they don't fit. Her favorite fans out when she twirls. She spins and spins on the kitchen floor because seeing the dress fan out makes her heart leap. I've watched her go from frustrated to joyful in a single moment, just by putting on this dress.

The Bible says we can get dressed up in something that will make our hearts leap too. God will present to us "a garment of praise instead of a spirit of despair" (Isa. 61:3 NIV). Like any garment, we have the choice to put it on.

Just like Esther did with her dress, we can ramp up our spirits by putting on praise.

If praise is a garment, then we have to put it on. Esther's twirly dress has never just jumped onto her body. Likewise, the garment of praise is something that we ultimately have to come into agreement with God about. Yes, he gave it to us and we have it in our possession, but we must use our free will to open our heart and praise him with intentionality. Praise initially may feel like a religious thing to do, but I want you to test this out for yourself. When you put on your garment of praise, you'll sense an uplifting within you! I will walk you through that experience in this chapter.

Dress Code

You wouldn't show up to the gym in formal attire, and you wouldn't attend a formal event in your gym clothes. Well, the space called REST also has a dress code. It is the garment of praise.

If you are serious about living in this precious space of REST, you must enter with the right attire. In this case, your attire is praise. Putting on praise is as simple as choosing to place your affection on God. Affection is "a gentle feeling of fondness or liking."[1] Where we place our affection becomes the thing we are most aware of. Many people say they don't feel God or know if he interacts with them. One simple way to become aware of his presence is to intentionally put your affection on him. It's truly incredible how wc can suddenly sense him; he's actually been there the whole time. This is a simple, intentional shift in where we place our affection.

Use Your Voice

Maybe you don't feel comfortable yet using your voice as we talked about earlier. That has to change! Your voice carries the power to change your world and the world. I'm serious. God spoke words to create the entire universe. The ground you are standing on was formed by words and only words. Words are so powerful—and not just God's words. Your words also carry life and death.

> The tongue can bring death or life;
>   those who love to talk will reap the consequences.
> (Prov. 18:21 NLT)

The Bible says that when God made humankind, he made us to be like him (see Gen. 1:26; 5:1). If God's words created the entire universe, then our words have creative power as well. And as you can see in the Scripture passage above, we will reap the consequences of the death or life that we speak.

I don't know about you, but it seems to me that it's easier to spray negative words into the atmosphere. But when it comes to positive words or praising God, we suddenly act as if we are speechless. Some of the most talkative people have the hardest time voicing their affection to God. You are about to see how effective your voice is for entering REST. As your voice expresses adoration to your King, you are dressing yourself in praise.

In the Ancient Roots Translinear Bible, Psalm 148:13 says to "catapult" God's name.

> Praise the name of Yahweh!
> Catapult his name and his majesty alone over the land
> and heaven.

Envision that you have words of affection for God loaded up in a catapult, and you launch them out into the atmosphere with your voice. Up and out they go, flying over your home, your business, your finances, your children, your marriage, your future, your neighborhood, and every part of your life. Your words are like confetti: they get everywhere and are very hard to remove. You can spray stinky confetti and reap the consequences of a stench that is difficult to remove, or you can catapult words of praise to a holy and loving God and watch them stick and change the atmosphere and your heart.

Let's put on the garment of praise. Find a quiet place where you can focus. In your own words, from your heart, write words to God that express your honest praise to him—your affection. (Some writing prompts include: "God, you are . . ." "You make me feel . . ." "I need you because . . ." "You are able to . . ." "You are bigger than . . ." "Your holiness feels like . . ." "Your majesty looks like . . ." "Thank you for . . .")

_____

_____

_____

_____

_____

_____

Now, go back and read your words out loud. Don't just read them; catapult them over God, yourself, your family, your job, your desires, your home, and your region. Read the words out loud as many times as you like.

Read the following psalm aloud to lift up your soul with praise. Circle or highlight the words and phrases that jump out at you. Meditate on those words. Let them marinate into your being and strengthen your soul in praise.

> Praise the LORD, my soul;
>> all my inmost being, praise his holy name.
> Praise the LORD, my soul,
>> and forget not all his benefits—

who forgives all your sins
and heals all your diseases,
who redeems your life from the pit
and crowns you with love and compassion,
who satisfies your desires with good things
so that your youth is renewed like the eagle's. (Ps.
103:1–5 NIV)

Congratulations, you just had a praise party (all dressed up in your garment of praise). Now, answer the same assessment question you did in the beginning of this chapter.

Right this second, I am feeling _____

_____.

Describe the shift you feel. In other words, what did putting on praise cause to shift within you? Do you feel more at REST?

_____

_____

_____

_____

_____

_____

_____

We recently released the *Still* video series, and the stories of what happened when groups put on praise are simply amazing.[2]

This is why church can be so much fun. If you attend a church that takes worship seriously, you will be led into your individual dressing room to put on your garment of praise.

I love our church because it's filled with true worshipers offering praise from their hearts. Worship isn't just music. Worship can be when we are eager to learn and lean into the sermon being preached because our affection is on Jesus. Worship can be when we allow our hearts to respond to someone telling the story of how God changed their life because our affection is on Jesus. Being generous with our time, talents, and money can be worship because we are expressing thankfulness to God for who he is and all he's given us. If our full affection has landed on Jesus, this is true worship.

Identity Makeover

While nursing my third baby in the middle of the night, I would watch *What Not to Wear*. The show goes like this: a person is nominated by a loved one to get a wardrobe makeover because the candidate has not learned to dress in a way that reveals their beauty. The fashion hosts surprise the candidate, who usually responds with embarrassment and hesitation, but all that subsides at the offer of a five-thousand-dollar shopping spree and makeover.

Once there is agreement, the stylists give the nominee an initial crash course on what would (and would not) flatter their figure. Afterward, the candidate is given the money and sent out shopping in high-end stores by themselves.

Nearly 100 percent of the time, the shopper has to be rescued by the stylists because they cannot bring themselves to buy anything in these high-end stores. They feel awkward dressing in fine clothing. It's not a money issue—they are gifted the money. It's an identity issue.

Right on time, the stylists begin helping them shop and telling them how great they look. They have the candidate stand in a three-way mirror and look at themselves—really look at themselves—and help them see their beauty in the right light. The stylists gush over beautiful attributes the person has never realized. Finally, they're sent to hair and makeup in preparation for their unveiling.

By the time of the big reveal, the made-over candidate feels over-the-top amazing about themselves. The entire process had to be forced on them because they couldn't initially see their own beauty, but by the end, they've experienced a complete identity makeover from the inside out.

Your Turn

The simplest way to describe identity is "how you see yourself." If you are having trouble showing your affection to God—getting dressed in the fancy clothing of verbal and expressive praise—it is most likely because you don't feel worthy to wear these garments of praise. Like the awkward shopper, you may feel out of sorts doing this for the first time.

How do you see yourself? Do you see yourself as worthy to enter the throne room of God and tell him how great he is? If not, please understand this: if you have given your life to the Lord Jesus Christ, then he has completely forgiven your sins. Our worthiness is not about perfection; it's about forgiveness. If you've been forgiven, you can have peace with God and be completely free from feeling one ounce of condemnation or shame. You are not a pauper or a slave but a daughter!

Meditate on the following Scripture passages until they become revealed truths to your spirit. Go ahead. Step into the three-way mirror and let God tell you some of the truths of who you are. As you believe what he says, you'll begin to feel more and more naturally beautiful wearing your garment of praise and royal crown.

> So now there is no longer any condemnation for those who believe in him, but the unbeliever already lives under condemnation because they do not believe in the name of God's beloved Son. (John 3:18)

> So now the case is closed. There remains no accusing voice of condemnation against those who are joined in life-union with Jesus, the Anointed One. (Rom. 8:1)

> Even though you were once distant from him, living in the shadows of your evil thoughts and actions, he reconnected you back to himself. He released his supernatural peace to you through the sacrifice of his own body as the sin-payment on your behalf so that you would dwell in his presence. And now there is nothing between you and Father God, for he sees you as holy, flawless, and restored, if indeed you continue to advance in faith, assured of a firm foundation to grow upon. Never be shaken from the hope of the gospel you have believed in. And this is the glorious news I preach all over the world. (Col. 1:21–23)

To practice this fourth way of finding REST, get out of bed in the morning and immediately put on the garment of praise. Like Esther, you can twirl your way through work, chores, projects, deadlines, and diapers. Remember that your RESTing place has a dress code. Throughout the day, add accessories of praise:

write a few sentences in your journal telling Jesus how much you love him, sing a song that lifts your spirits while folding laundry, thank him for your children as you put their clothes away, or express your gratitude to the Lord for helping you get through a presentation at work. Catapult God's name over your work, your duties, and all your responsibilities. "Lord, I praise you for this project. Thank you for helping me." You may not feel like getting dressed up, but the rewards in your spirit will be worth it.

Dressing yourself in constant expressions of praise is one of the fastest ways to enter the place of REST!

15

WAY 5

LIVE IN THE PRESENT
IN GOD'S PRESENCE AND POWER

y little Esther pulled a children's book off the shelf and began to read it aloud. From the kitchen, I overheard something like this:

Make your bed! Hurry up! Hurry up!
Eat your cereal! Hurry up! Hurry up!
Run to school! Hurry up! Hurry up!

I made a beeline for the living room and snatched the book out of her hands. As a recovering hurry-upper, I didn't want my kids to fall into that habit. I thought about getting rid of the book, but I knew I would need it to prove a point one day. That day is today.

The book conveys an innocent idea and is rather descriptive of how most families live. Is it any wonder we are more anxious than any other generation that has come before us? We are living in a world that screams, "Hurry up! Hurry up!" This revs our mental engines, and we blow past our lives. Hours turn to years, and suddenly we realize that we have hurried our way through life so much that we have missed most of it.

As we were getting off a flight recently, a man scolded another passenger who he thought wasn't getting his luggage from the overhead compartment fast enough. He couldn't wait an extra ten seconds and actually cursed at the guy. I asked Bob what he thought about the scene the guy made, and he said, "It's the condition of our culture. Selfishness. I feel bad for the guy." I pray that people who have bought into the lie that they must live their lives in a hurry will hurry up and read this book (joking). But seriously, this hurry-up virus is very easy to catch.

The other day I was talking with someone and felt I needed to get going. And then I thought, *Why do I feel like I need to rush off? I enjoy spending time with this person. I am enjoying our conversation, and there isn't anywhere I have to be.*

I caught myself in the act of hurrying for the sake of hurrying. I didn't look like I was in a hurry like the guy on the plane, but my thoughts were badgering me forward for no good reason. The hurry bug can deplete our REST.

I realized I hurry because I feel like that's what I'm supposed to do—rush off to the next thing. As a culture, we are in a hurry. Fast food isn't fast enough. High speed internet isn't speedy enough. And it is certainly taking me too long to write this book.

Sigh.

"But, Jenny, I'm in a hurry to get to my goals!" Yes, that is fine and good, as long as you are living in God's rhythm for your life. In Psalm 139:16, God says that he designed all our days before we were born.

You Are a Human Be-ing

A few years ago, I was confronted with my hurry-up habit. What I have discovered is that some of us build the hurry-up habit subconsciously during those times when we are stressed or overwhelmed with all we need to accomplish in what seems like too little time. Exercise, cleaning the house, or whatever it is that feels emotionally or physically draining can pull our hurry-up trigger. And don't even get me started with getting the kids out the door for school or church.

Am I suggesting we lollygag through life? No way! There is a lot to accomplish in a day. But I can tell you that you can move with speed and productivity without a frazzled mind, which absolutely steals our REST. REST means that we are RESTing in what is happening right this second with a complete trust that God will meet us in our next moment. We can let go of turning things over and over in our minds, knowing that God will be there when we get to those things. We can REST in the right now, even if it's a moment we don't want to be in. We can relax and be.

We are conditioned to do-ing, so be-ing can be challenging. Our minds become jammed freeways of thoughts concerning all the things we need to do. When we get stuck in these mental traffic jams, we end up missing moments. Did you know that our physical bodies can be in one place while our minds are somewhere entirely different?

Have any of these ever happened to you?

- Someone is talking to you, but your mind is thinking about a looming deadline.
- You are tucking the kids in bed, but your mind is on the lunches and house chores you still need to get to.
- You are exercising, but you're watching the clock like a hawk, wishing the minutes would go by faster.
- You are talking to your spouse, but you grab your phone every time it buzzes or lights up.
- You are in a conversation with a friend, but your eyes are wandering all over the place because you can't disconnect from what's happening around you.

Think about all we miss in each of these situations because we aren't really there.

Working from a Place of REST

Oddly, my REST training came to a crescendo on a spin bike of all places. A spin bike became the place where God asked me to completely kill the hurry-up monster that had been haunting me. He wanted me to be 100 percent present in the moment. I had to learn to be. I would have to resist looking at the clock or wishing away the time. He wanted me to fully engage: feel the burn, listen to my breath, and feel a drop of sweat trickle down my face. He was teaching me to find peace in a place where peace wasn't naturally found. Remember the tornado? He was walking me into the outer vortex of the tornado and guiding me into the center to claim my territory of total REST and peace on the inside. He was teaching me to be still inside and to work at the same time. He was teaching me how to work from a place of REST.

I spent two years on the bike practicing being present in God's presence, and it has completely changed my life. (See the appendix for a step-by-step guide to REST training through the mode of exercise. The steps can also be duplicated in other activities.) This is the vital thrust through the door to REST along our journey. To find REST, we must practice being right here in whatever conditions that we find ourselves.

Take a moment right now. Pause. Listen to the sounds around you. What do you hear? Ambient noise? White noise? Notice what you didn't notice before. Now, become fully aware of your body. How do your muscles feel? Are you clenching a part of your body or are you hunched up unconsciously? Take sixty seconds to fully embrace this moment.

During the sixty seconds, did you find yourself RESTing? Perhaps you found yourself trying to hurry the sixty seconds along. That's okay. It took me several practice sessions on the bike to overcome the hurry-up mind-set that I didn't even realize was bullying me. Once you get this down, it will become a daily habit. Even now, I have to walk myself through the process and find the center—the pocket of REST.

To Wish Away the Time Is to Wish Away Your REST

During my time on the bike, I discovered that long, deep breaths were the key to bringing my mind into the present. I would close my eyes and count one hundred deep inhales and exhales while listening to their rhythm. As I would draw air deep into my belly and exhale slowly, I would begin to become anchored.

Distractions would fall away, and I would begin to focus on what was happening right that second.

When I first started this practice, I was tempted to look at the time and think, "I have only ten minutes left." I realized that wishing away the time was a natural response to the pain that is naturally felt during exercise. I called this pain the resistance. I wanted it to be over with. But God was guiding me into a place where REST was available in the middle of the resistance, in the middle of the storm.

As I continued to practice being present in God's presence, the pocket became easier for me to find and I found it more quickly. My rides started to become euphoric, in fact, and I felt as if I could pedal forever. Sometimes I would glance at my heart rate in disbelief because I was certain I must have slowed down, but I hadn't. Sometimes quite the contrary. Yet I was so peaceful.

Over time I learned how to become aware when I was wishing away the time, not only on my bike but also in my day-to-day life. I had to become extremely aware of that sensation because wishing away the time was one of the things that most quickly threw me out of the pocket and out of REST. Throughout the day when I would catch myself trying to escape the present, I would breathe in, re-anchor my thoughts, and gather my mind back to the moment I was in.

Before discovering that my greatest peace and energy could be found in the present moment, I had been trained to use hurrying and stress as my energy sources; they were old ways of fueling myself. When I learned to be present and to welcome God's presence, I exchanged my hurry and worry for the tangible surges of RESTful energy that I received from God in the right here and the right now.

I would be thrilled for you to find this pocket. There is nothing like it. It is found in the presence of God.

Worry Isn't Worth It

Answer this question: Do you find yourself worrying? About what? Write down your thoughts.

_____

_____

_____

_____

_____

As normal as worry feels, it's a sin. I don't say this to condemn you but to set you free. Sin is not fun that God is trying to withhold from us. Rather, it is something he knows will harm us.

Do you roll things over in your mind? Should I have done that? Maybe I should have said that differently? I wonder what she's going to act like the next time we're together? These kinds of worrisome thoughts will wear you down. There is no REST in worry.

> Therefore I tell you, do not worry about your life, what you will eat or drink; or about your body, what you will wear. Is not life more than food, and the body more than clothes? Look at the birds of the air; they do not sow or reap or store away in barns, and yet your heavenly Father feeds them. Are you not much more valuable than they? Can any one of you by worrying add a single hour to your life? (Matt. 6:25–27 NIV)

Living in worry will steal your REST.

Have you ever been so nervous about an upcoming event that you played the potential scenarios over and over in your mind? This is especially common if you're embarking on something new or if you don't like unknowns (most of us don't).

The first time I was invited to speak in public I was so nervous. I was turning the event over and over in my mind, which was keeping my anxiety stirred up. I began to pray that God would help me overcome the worry I was experiencing.

Hannah, my oldest daughter, was about five at the time. She handed me a picture she had drawn in which I was pulling a roller bag behind me. Another girl was following me, pulling a bag too. Above my head was the label "Mom," and over the other person's head she had written "Grace." When I asked her what the picture meant, she said, "Grace is going with you on your trip." My spirit jumped; I knew that grace was my answer. I began to dig further into what the grace of God really meant. Here's what I found: grace is an actual presence—the presence of God. It is the supernatural empowerment that is provided at the exact moment we need it and to the exact measure we need it.

For example, if you need the grace (supernatural empowerment) to work a double shift, you will receive that power at the exact moment you are working the double shift, not when you are *thinking* about doing it.

If you are meeting a friend for a difficult conversation, you can turn it over and over in your mind and try to play out the conversation, but what a waste of time and joy. Instead, because of God's grace, you can simply thank God for the grace that is going to show up. Ask him for wisdom and love for the meeting and forget about it. God's grace will meet you there.

When we mentally obsess about the future and try to live out a moment before we are in it, we anticipate what that moment might feel like without the benefit of the grace of God. We assume it will be difficult—and we haven't even done anything yet. The grace of God we need to do anything at all in life will be available exactly when we need it. Overanalyzing our lives or letting our imagination run wild will never create peace. If we are living in the future and not the present, we're creating dread; if we are living in the past, we're creating regret.

Grace—Our Daily Bread

Grace is substance. Grace is our daily bread. Grace is the presence and provision of God. It provides energy and satisfaction for the current moment. The Bible contains several accounts of God showing up for the Israelites at the exact moment they were in need. After they escaped from slavery in Egypt and entered the wilderness, they didn't have food. So God created manna, a type of bread-like substance that showed up on the ground every morning. Manna had all the nutrition they needed. The catch was that manna spoiled after one day, so they couldn't store leftovers. They had to trust God to show up every morning with supernatural food for forty years! That's a dramatic picture of grace. It shows up at the exact moment we need it, in the right quantity, and the contents are exactly what we need. But we cannot store up today's grace for tomorrow. We need to trust God to provide a new, fresh batch of grace for the demands of tomorrow.

Today is the most important day of our lives because it is the only day we are living in. God, however, exists outside of time. He is not limited to today, so he already has our tomorrow stocked up with all the grace we're going to need. We, on the other hand, are limited by time. We can't use today's grace for tomorrow's race. Save yourself the trouble of getting overly consumed about tomorrow. God is already there.

Expecting God to provide you with what you will need always comes back to trust—trusting in God, your Father. You are a daughter of God, so it's safe to go ahead and lean into him and let go of tomorrow. No more separation anxiety, remember? The root of anxiety is being separated from his presence, but you are not separated from his presence anymore. You can REST, knowing that he has enough grace, enough supernatural empowerment, to help you over the hurdles of tomorrow.

He Is Our Power Source

Have you ever looked back on a difficult season of your life and said, "I don't know how I did that." The answer is that you were supernaturally empowered by God. This is grace! God sourced you with the energy, power, intellect, gifting, skill set, passion, drive, and love that it took for you to make it through that challenging time of your life.

The most common reaction I get from people when they find out I have five kids, run a large business, run a nonprofit, and minister with my husband at our church is, "I don't know how you do that." I can promise you it's not in my own strength. God puts his grace manna on my ground when I wake up every morning, and I receive its nutrition.

Maybe some of you question whether God is helping you out in this supernatural way because you haven't felt the grace I'm speaking of. Could it be that you simply don't notice it?

Perhaps it's hidden in plain sight, like that drink packet in my kitchen drawer.

The Bible says that all who believe in the name of Jesus can have the Holy Spirit come upon them with power. His power doesn't come through our own strength or our lists of do's and don'ts. His power comes through his Holy Spirit. To be empowered, all we need to do is connect to his Spirit, much like plugging a dead phone into a charger. When we are connected to him, we become sourced with all the power we need for the moment we're in.

Which attributes of God are you most desperate for and in need of today? Do you need patience, creativity, love? Choose as many as you want. Next to each one, write down the reason or the scenario in your life that requires this part of who he is. For example, my back was injured a few weeks ago. I was in agonizing pain and discovered I had a compression fracture in my spine. I called upon the healing attribute of God. He healed me over the course of a few days. This is what I mean by God being our source for everything we need, large or small.

Inseparable

Nothing can separate us from the love of God.

When I teach about how inseparable we are from God's love, I like to demonstrate it using red and blue playdough: the blue represents our state without God; the red represents the blood that was shed by Jesus. Because Jesus shed his blood to reconcile us to God, when someone puts their trust in him, they become connected to God—so I mash the two colors together. Next, I hand the now purple ball of playdough to someone watching and say, "Let's say this person who became one with God gets really distracted and stops praying and reading their Bible. They lose their energy for God. They are still fond of God, but they feel like God is probably not happy with them and has decided to leave them alone for the time being. Would you please separate the two colors of playdough to represent this separation?" You can imagine the response from the person holding the single purple ball of dough.

Obviously, the ball of purple playdough is never going to go back to a ball of blue and a ball of red. When we say yes to Jesus, we say yes to a color blend. We are now walking around in purple, which represents royalty. Whatever is in Jesus is now in us. Jesus, who is God, has allowed us to blend with our Father God. We blend into intimacy.

> So now I live with the confidence that there is nothing in the universe with the power to separate us from God's love. I'm convinced that his love will triumph over death, life's troubles, fallen angels, or dark rulers in the heavens. There is nothing in our present or future circumstances that can weaken his love. (Rom. 8:38)

Time to Fill Up

Take the last moments of this chapter to REST in God's power and presence. Find a quiet place where you won't be interrupted and where you can physically relax your entire body. Ask him aloud to fill you up and drench you with his Holy Spirit. Start by taking a deep breath into the deepest part of your abdomen. Exhale slowly. Count one hundred breaths. Focus your mind on this moment. Listen to your breath. As you breathe, breathe in the Holy Spirit. Invite him to fill up your body to overflowing. You may feel a sensation of power, possibly electricity, and maybe slight shaking. Resist judging your experience. Let it be what it is. Breathe in his love. Remember that he has forgiven you so that he can be with you and love you. He wants to be with you. Breathe. Breathe. Breathe him in.

To practice this fifth way of finding REST, develop the habit, after waking, of breathing deeply and exhaling deeply before starting your day. Count one hundred breaths, pulling your mind to the present moment. When you inhale, inhale God's presence. The Holy Spirit is the Spirit of God, and as a believer, you have access to all that God is 24/7. Throughout your day, anytime you catch yourself wishing away the time, breathe in his peace and exhale your worry. This is a new life pattern that will allow you to live in REST.

There is nothing more energizing, powerful, and life giving than living presently in the presence and the power of God.

16

WAY 6

ENTER THE GARDEN

As my first baby, Hannah, slept quietly in her car seat, I pulled into the driveway of a client's house to meet about her business. I will never forget how confused I felt as to whether or not to bring baby Hannah in. I was stumped. Could my sleeping newborn be in a business meeting? I couldn't make heads or tails of my situation, so I stood at the front door talking to my friend while keeping one eye on the car in the driveway.

Fifteen years later, I giggle about this because I had no clue how to mesh these two worlds—motherhood and business—even when I was literally my own boss.

I used to live my life in compartments. I had heard successful people say that, as women, we wear many hats, so it seemed like the right thing to do.

Be a mom.

Now, be a businesswoman.

Okay, go back to mom.

Hurry, go be a friend.

Wait, your husband needs you.

It feels a bit like learning to drive a stick shift.

I bought into this hat thing for a while, but I became exhausted and intimidated by my own schedule. I would go to bed with a heavy spirit of dread, running a dress rehearsal for the rapid costume changes I had ahead of me the next day. I was exhausted just thinking about it, let alone living it out.

Christine, a minister at my church and now a dear friend, scooped me up and began pouring into me. She taught me to go to my prayer closet, my Bible, and my Jesus for absolutely everything. Sitting in her living room during one prayer meeting, I remember her telling the group that she was a daughter. That was her identity. Everything she did flowed from that place. I had to chew on that because being a daughter was foreign to me.

I wanted to be a daughter, but I didn't know how. I had attached my identity to do-ing, not be-ing.

It took me a while, but I stepped awkwardly into my daughter role with God and asked him to help me figure it out. He knew this was a clumsy place for me.

> "I will be a true Father to you,
>   and you will be my beloved sons and daughters,"
>   says the Lord Yahweh Almighty. (2 Cor. 6:18)

I'm here to tell you that you don't wear many hats. You wear a crown. The crown is engraved "daughter."

Imagine you are standing in a boat in the middle of the ocean. Your boat is full, and as you add more things to the boat, it begins to gradually press down into the water until water starts to fill the inside. There is too much stuff in the boat. What is the next logical step? Grab what seems to have the least value and toss it overboard. If the boat goes down, so will you, along with everything in it.

The boat represents our capacity for life. For me, it used to be sixteen waking hours. Whatever fit in sixteen hours was all there was room for. My old boat was a rigid sixteen-hour boat that I had to cram as much stuff into as I could. But I found that sixteen hours a day were never enough. When I came into the revelation of REST, I realized that the problem was not all the stuff I was putting in the boat but the boat itself—a rigid and inflexible box.

As I learned to REST, my boat paradigm was replaced by the image of a garden—a completely different landscape. My capacity was no longer defined by a sixteen-hour clock or the amount of energy I could muster up in that time period. The Lord invited me into a new landscape—one with no walls.

The Gardener

As it turns out, I'm not on a boat after all. I'm in a garden. The Master Gardener is in my garden pulling weeds, tilling soil, planting new species that I've never seen before, and there is also a lot of pruning going on. It is messy, but really beautiful at the same time. I am not in charge of the garden. If something gets pruned back, it's because the Gardener knows it is best to cut that friendship or project or mind-set back for a moment so I can bear more fruit. If a new species is planted, I explore it with wonder and excitement, having no idea what it will grow up to look like at full bloom. The weeding sometimes surprises me because what I thought was a flower is actually a weed that needs to go. I don't need to argue or stress in my garden because it isn't mine to maintain.

Abide on the Vine

In one famous analogy, Jesus referred to himself as the vine and described us as his branches. Our role is simply to abide as he lives through us. In contrast, a branch disconnected from the vine cannot do anything because no life is being pumped to it.

> I am the sprouting vine and you're my branches. As you live in union with me as your source, fruitfulness will stream from within you—but when you live separated from me you are powerless. (John 15:5)

To abide is to remain. If we remain connected to God, then life will continually be pumping in and through us. It is a 24/7 reliance on God, who is good and kind and has fruit that he wants to produce through us.

How do we translate garden living into a Monday? How do we abide on the vine in the midst of the mundane? We do this by inviting Jesus, the Master Gardener, into everything we do. Ask Jesus to come to work with you. Invite him to do the dishes with you. When you are a taxi mom, have him join you on the trip. Don't limit your time with him to a mealtime prayer. To abide means to remain. When we remain in him, we will bear much fruit.

FTO

It's Monday. You are working. You're connected to Jesus all day, and God starts talking to you. He wants to partner with you in working out some great things through your life. He begins to give you instruction, and . . .

This is where I see people trip into the biggest pothole on their way toward a fruitful life in God. When the Gardener gives you instructions, it's in your best interest to obey, not because God is going to be outraged with you if you don't but because he has more for you. That "more" is a product of obedience. He is trying to grow some big fat fruit on your branches.

Today is Valentine's Day. I have candy and a few goodies waiting for my kids when they get home from school. When they come through the door, I'll say, "Happy Valentine's Day! These goodies are for you. Come to the table and see what I got you." I can predict with 100 percent accuracy that they're not going to hesitate. It's easy to "obey" your parents when there is immediate gratification from doing so.

However, at dinner I might have to ask them three times to eat their vegetables. Either they are experiencing sudden hearing loss or they are disobeying me. When I say, "Eat your vegetables," am I trying to torture my kids and make them suffer? No! I want to make sure they get some fiber and vitamins in their bodies. It's not as easy to obey when we're being asked to do something we don't want to do.

We have a term in our house called FTO: first time obedience. We learned this phrase from our great friends Danny and Diane. They've been a gift to us for parenting wisdom. From them we learned that obedience is a first time thing. The first time Bob and I tell our kids to do something, we expect them to obey. When it comes to going out for ice cream, they have FTO down! When it comes to eating broccoli, doing the dishes, and cleaning their rooms? We're still working on that.

Why is it loving for Bob and me to take the time and energy to teach our kids to obey when we tell them to clean their rooms or take their vitamins? Because we're preparing them for what we know is coming. When we send them into the world, we obviously want them to know these life skills. But the greater goal is the development of a humble heart that is willing to respect and obey authority—and ultimately God. If they don't learn this, they will soon be fired from any job. If they want to lead others, they must first learn to obey a leader. Of course, they are too young to understand now, but this will matter for their future. For now, I just look like a maniac chasing them around with vitamins. It would be so much easier on me not to do any of this, but because I love and care for them so much, I am uncompromising that they learn to obey.

So let's get a bit personal. When God asks you to do something or stop doing something, what is your initial thought? Are you good at FTO? When God prompts you to do something you don't really want to do—forgive an offender, serve someone in need, work on a challenging project, apologize for hurting someone, quit an addiction—do you have FTO? Or do you rationalize, negotiate, procrastinate, or just ignore it altogether?

God gives a great deal of instruction in the Bible. He calls for obedience when it comes to being generous, being humble, serving one another, being faithful, trusting him rather than being anxious, and so on. Sometimes we view God like my kids probably view me—as someone who has rules that don't make any sense or don't please our senses. However, as any parent will understand, FTO in our relationship with God will change our lives, and disobedience will too.

Obedience brings REST. Disobedience brings anxiety.

The most fundamental root belief that will get your obedience muscles moving is knowing deep within you that God is not a taskmaster. He is good. Read that again. *He is good.* He is entirely light; no darkness can come from him. It is impossible for him to guide his sheep astray.

So why is obedience so difficult?

The Bible refers to an internal war being waged within us 24/7, like two cats in a bag.

> Through my experience of this principle, I discover that even when I want to do good, evil is ready to sabotage me. Truly, deep within my true identity, I love to do what pleases God. But I discern another power operating in my humanity, waging a war against the moral principles of my conscience and bringing me into captivity as a prisoner to the "law" of sin—this unwelcome intruder in my humanity. (Rom. 7:21–23)

The spirit, the part of us constantly communing with God, can hear God's instruction and immediately know the right thing to do. The flesh, the self-centered part of us that craves immediate satisfaction and comfort, says, "Excuse me? I am not doing that. Here are eighteen reasons why that doesn't make any sense."

If we continue to feed the flesh whatever it demands, it will become bigger and puffier than the spirit and, after a while, overshadow and outshout the spirit like an attention-starved toddler or a dominating party guest. This is when we experience a tug-of-war in our emotions.

The soul isn't bad. It was given to us by God and contains our personality and emotions. That said, the main role of the soul is to be the unique expression of the spirit. When the spirit is leading the soul, the soul becomes a beautiful, fruitful expression of the spirit that lives within us. The soul was never designed to lead. Having the soul in front is like my three-year-old leading my home. Yikes.

Your spirit is the leader, connected to God's Spirit, and your soul can be nurtured by your spirit, expressing what it gets from God.

From Bending to Breaking

Obedience to God is the antidote to overfed flesh. Each time we choose to obey, we deflate the size of the flesh's inherently selfish appetite.

Fasting is another way to amplify the spirit over the flesh. Fasting is critical to the Christian walk because we can all let our souls grow out of control at times. Fasting denies our physical bodies food and is helpful because naturally, in overabundance, food causes us to crave more and more food that may not be best for us. When we fast, we also deny the unhealthy appetites within us such as our desire to compare, become jealous, lust, get angry, and so on. When we fast, those appetites no longer have the tenacity and strength to overtake us.

I have come to realize that some things only bend in prayer but will break through fasting. Do you have a stubborn soul talking you out of your destiny? Do you have a soul that seems to dominate your courage and put you in a place of weakness? If you find it difficult to obey because of doubts and unbelief, it's time to fast. Fasting is like putting my three-year-old in her appropriate role and taking away some of the privileges she doesn't deserve. Sometimes not just our souls need fasting but also scenarios that just aren't budging through prayer. Fasting is a powerful and spiritual force that breaks those things that are only bending.

For instance, throughout the writing of this book, I was on a water fast. The Lord told me that what he taught me about REST was not mine to keep but mine to release. However, prior to my fast, I couldn't seem to get the right words on the paper. I would type, then doubt, and questions would bombard me. I would shut my laptop and walk away. When I entered my fast, I had twenty-five pages written. By day nine, I had written 90 percent of the book. For me, it was a night and day difference.

Fasting should always be done with prayer. Fasting without prayer is just going hungry.

Again using the example of this book, I prayed and called on a group of friends to pray with and for me. I asked them to encircle me in prayer so that this book would get written. Without their prayers and fasting, I am positive this book would not have come to pass in the manner that it has. I am so grateful.

Do you have friends you can call on to pray with and for you? Do you have a willingness to fast in order to break through some stubborn challenges?

People often ask me how to fast. There are many ways it can be done. First and foremost, obey what your spirit says to do.

If you are new to fasting, a Daniel fast may be a great place to start. (You can search for this online.) Daniel was a mighty man of God who ate only vegetables and fruit for ten days and in the end proved to be stronger than any of the men who ate everything they wanted.

Water fasts can range from one day to several weeks. A three-day fast will cause toxins to be released from fat cells. Consult a physician if you are under care for a medical condition before attempting a fast.

Humility—Whee!

Obedience and fasting and prayer require humility—laying down our own way to submit to God's way. Humility brings acceleration in our kingdom work like a greased up Slip 'N Slide, launching us into what God has for us as quickly as he deems possible. Pride, on the other hand, is like jumping with all our might onto a dry Slip 'N Slide. It's going to hurt. I suppose that's why the Bible says that pride comes before a fall.

Humility is not synonymous with being quiet or playing life safe. Humility is submitting to the Gardener's will and timing, believing he knows how to produce a rich harvest within our garden better than we do. He has many plans for us to bear fruit and feed the world with the good things that come from us, but without humble obedience, we may get only as far as a potted plant in a windowsill.

When we humble ourselves, life gets a lot more fun because we don't have the pressure of needing to have all the answers. When I have a difficult project in front of me, I am not shy about calling up a friend and asking for help. We have work parties and team up to get the job done. I've made my closest friends this way. With humility at work between us, we can work together for a common mission. The same is true with God. He isn't asking us to go it alone. He's inviting us to come along. Obey and watch your garden begin to flourish.

You show that you are my intimate friends when you obey all that I command you. I have never called you "servants," because a master doesn't confide in his servants, and servants don't always understand what the master is doing. But I call you my most intimate friends, for I reveal to you everything that I've heard from my Father. You didn't choose me, but I've chosen and commissioned you to go into the world to bear fruit. And your fruit will last, because whatever you ask of my Father, for my sake, he will give it to you! So this is my parting command: Love one another deeply! (John 15:14–17)

Jesus's charge to us is to love one another. When we refuse to love someone, we prove that we are not in fellowship with God. In fact, of the directives God gave us in the Bible, he said love was the greatest of them all.

"Teacher, which commandment in the law is the greatest?" Jesus answered him, "'Love the Lord your God with every passion of your heart, with all the energy of your being, and with every thought that is within you.' This is the great and supreme commandment. And the second is like it in importance: 'You must love your friend in the same way you love yourself.'" (Matt. 22:36–39)

Love Is Premium Fuel

I am a worker. I am a driver. I love working hard, then stepping back to see my flourishing garden. Maybe you are like that? My question is, What fuels you to work and labor?

My go-to fuel used to be a cheap fill-up of stress. I would grab the stress hose, fill up, and off I'd go. Oddly, stress got me down the road a bit. But cheap fuel causes our engines to wear out faster.

What fuel do you reach for when the pressure is on or a goal has been set in front of you? Cheap fuel can be jealousy, insecurity, anger, self-pity, fear of failure. There are plenty of cheap fuels that may work for a time, but each will ultimately steal your REST.

This is why we need to begin to walk hand in hand with the Gardener. He is REST. He is love. His love is premium fuel. When we find the pocket of REST, we simply trust the Father to lead the way.

I love each of you with the same love that the Father loves me. You must continually let my love nourish your hearts. If you keep my commands, you will live in my love, just as I have kept my Father's commands, for I continually live nourished and empowered by his love. My purpose for telling you these things is so that the joy that I experience will fill your hearts with overflowing gladness! So this is my command: Love each other deeply, as much as I have loved you. For the greatest love of all is a love that sacrifices all. And this great love is demonstrated when a person sacrifices his life for his friends. (John 15:9–13)

What is your go-to fuel? Write down your thoughts.

_____

_____

_____

Could you make a conscious decision to put your faith in God to tend your garden and in his love to fuel you?

To practice this sixth way of finding REST, start tomorrow with a garden under your feet. You are being fueled to accomplish all your duties by the love of God. Choose love to fill up your tank in the morning. Ask God throughout the day to help you work from a place of REST. Invite him into all your responsibilities and grant him permission to garden away. Ask him to bless you.

If you feel led to fast for a day this week, try it. You may choose half a day or maybe three days. There is no one right way. The goal is to let him be your vine, your nourishment, even if you are simply skipping one meal.

May God bless you as you allow him to grow, prune, plant, and water your garden. This is RESTing in his care.

17

WAY 7
WRESTLE INTO REST

*Y*ou've learned about six ways that lead to REST. Well done! You've been . . .

leaning into God
letting go and trusting God with your life
cultivating intimacy with God
putting on the garment of praise
living in the present in God's presence and power
and entering the garden, abiding with the Gardener

The last way will prepare us for the battles for REST that lie ahead. Don't let this knowledge discourage you, but storms are coming. How do I know this? Jesus guaranteed it.

And everything I've taught you is so that the peace which is in me will be in you and will give you great confidence as you rest in me. For in this unbelieving world you will experience trouble and sorrows, but you must be courageous, for I have conquered the world! (John 16:33)

At times, we are going to lose our REST. Challenges come. Tragedies hit. And we find ourselves coiled up in unREST. At those times, we need to wrestle into REST.

The Resistance

This was my before-church experience about two months ago, play-by-play.

Mom is late for church. Dad is already there.
Mom asks kids multiple times to get in car.
Kids are all finally in car.
Mom leaves driveway and heads to church.
Smallest kid throws up breakfast in car seat.
Kids scream.
Teenager rolls down windows to air out car.
Other kids scream to roll up windows because they are freezing.
Mom asks teenager a question and teenager puts earbuds in.
Mom loses it.
Mom aggressively yanks earbuds out of teenager's ears.
Mom doesn't want to go to church anymore.
Then Mom remembers she's a minister at church.
Mom painfully pulls into church parking lot.
Dad texts Mom from inside the building. "Are you coming in?"
"Maybe."

Mom cries.
Mom feels a little better.
Mom remembers kid in car seat covered in vomit.
Mom takes deep breath.
Mom gets baby out of car.
Mom asks Holy Spirit for help.
Holy Spirit reminds Mom that she has an extra shirt in her bag for vomit baby.
Mom thanks God for this miracle.
Mom thanks God for her children.
Holy Spirit tells Mom she doesn't need to rush.
Mom takes her time to change baby.
Mom asks God to please fix mess with teenager.
Mom doesn't understand teenager.
Teenager doesn't understand Mom.
Mom walks into worship.
The words and music wash over Mom.
Mom hears life-giving message on love.
The words give oxygen to Mom's spirit.
Mom thanks God for the Word and for teenager.
Mom asks God to refresh her relationship with her kids.
Mom admits she blew it.
Mom asks God to help her.
Mom releases the stress and guilt.
Mom asks teenager to forgive her.
Mom hugs teenager and moves on with the rest of her day.

As much as I'd like to tell you that you will live in uninterrupted REST for the rest of your life, it's just not true. I still find myself, at times, frazzled over or frustrated with people, situations, or my own issues. I find myself wanting to control my kids or Bob and get my way. As frustrating as these times can be, the important thing is to get back on the road to REST.

On-Ramp to REST

A few years ago, I left a friend's house with five kids in my car for a sleepover. It was midnight, and I had to drive across Portland back to my house. Out of fear of missing a freeway connection, I accidentally took an exit too soon. Suddenly, I was driving down the most disturbing street in our city. The kids' eyes were peeled watching the people walk up and down the strip. And of course, my phone died. No charger. "Okay," I said, maintaining my peace, "just turn around and merge back onto the freeway." I calmly entered my address into my car's navigation system. The only problem was that when I drove back toward the freeway, there was no on-ramp. I began to drive in a large, one-mile loop over and over as the voice chirped, "Do a U-turn. Do a U-turn." My navigation system appeared to be as lost as I was.

A child in the backseat said, "Ms. Jenny, you live a long ways away." We'd been looping for thirty minutes, and I was about to lose my mind. Where was the road that would get me back on the freeway? Stress was mounting as I became more and more aware that my friends' precious children were now getting an unintended education on Portland's night life. Knowing that every road eventually connects to the freeway, I decided to use my mind rather than rely on technology. I started driving in the general direction of the freeway and settled into peace. I took turns down side streets until I found an on-ramp.

In the same way, we can veer off the road of REST and find ourselves looping around in unREST for hours, days, or months. The fact is that you *will* find yourself in the corrupted streets of unREST, and you won't like it. You may do a few loops, but I'm here to tell you that you have a choice: continue to loop around in unREST, remaining stressed, angry, anxious, or hurt, or get on the on-ramp and get the heck out of there!

Here are turn-by-turn navigation instructions to help you find the on-ramp. You have to want to get back into REST and to win the battle you are in. Don't be a victim. Position yourself as a victor and make your way back to the main road that leads to REST.

First: R-elease E-very S-ingle T-hing

Pride and control lead us off the exit to unREST: "I must take control." Humility and trust lead us to the on ramp back to REST: "I will release control."

I jumped into the car to grab takeout for my family. I left the house frustrated because I had been having a highly agitating conversation with one of my kids. We were nitpicking each other, and it was only getting worse.

As I drove away from the house, I could feel my insides knotting up in unREST. I admitted, "Lord, I don't know how to help her. I am totally beside myself about what to do."

Immediately, I heard, "REST."

"Okay, I'll REST. But I'm really frazzled, so walk me through this."

Then I heard, "Release Every Single Thing."

God was asking me to release her, in other words, to let go.

In my brain, I already knew this. But it became real within my heart as I drove to the restaurant. I breathed in deeply, receiving fuel from my love source, and breathed out my daughter. I released her.

I immediately felt a release. My Father God wasn't telling me to fix anything. His greatest commandment is to love—this was my only job. The increase, the growth, the pruning of our relationship was in his hands. I asked for wisdom concerning how to be the mom she needed me to be. I hadn't parented a teenager before, so I needed wisdom, stat!

God took me back to the garden.

I imagined the Father dressed as a gardener. He had on rubber gloves and an apron. He was working diligently on a complex plant that looked like a mess of thorns and flowers. It was not quite clear what he was shaping or what his strategy was, but he clearly had a plan. His focus was impeccable. The only thing I knew to do was stand back and watch the plant take shape. I didn't know how to help even if I could.

What situation or emotion are you facing that feels complex and confusing? What stronghold is grinding at you and stealing your peace, causing you to loop in unREST? Write down your thoughts.

_____

_____

_____

_____

_____

Take a moment to breathe in the love and concern of God for these matters. Now, breathe out control. See yourself humbly handing over the reins of the matter while you step back and allow God to battle for you. Soften your heart and breathe out control a few more times until you feel the unREST melt in the hands of God.

Second: See with Love and Walk in Wisdom

Releasing something or someone to God doesn't mean we can ignore the fact that a problem exists. If we want to win the battle we're in, we must see through God's eyes of love and walk in his wisdom. Catch this in your spirit: see with love, walk in wisdom.

With love (or without love) is how we see people and situations. Ask the Lord to give you his perspective for people. Borrow his eyes and see with his heart. God sees people with a strong affection for how he made them, regardless of how they are acting. It's no easy task to see people the way God does. It's easier to see people in light of their behavior rather than their God-given nature. But we can't treat people with love if we see them as idiots, incapable, undeserving, or irritating.

The ability to see people the way God sees them will grease the unREST we have for them in our hearts, and the icky-sticky judgment crud will begin to slide away. A heart full of judgment and offense (unforgiveness) is an enemy—an arrester—of our REST.

Ask God right now to help you see people, even the most irritating and hard to love people, in light of his heart for them.

God, I release my eyes and heart to you. I surrender my own critical view of people and myself and receive your sight. I want to see people as you see them. God, give me correct sight for _____ , as I have had a hard time loving them.

Forgive me for judging them and seeing them in light of their
weaknesses. Amen.

Say this prayer, with a genuine heart, for as many people as
you need to, as many times as you need to.

With wisdom (or without wisdom) is how we deal with
people and situations. Take a look at this proverb:

> If you solicit good advice, then your plans will
>   succeed.
> So don't charge into battle without wisdom,
> for wars are won by skillful strategy. (Prov. 20:18)

Walking in wisdom begins when we hand over our egos and
desire to be the god of our own lives. The Bible says that God
wants to give us wisdom. In other words, we need to plug in
our navigation system, swallow our pride, and follow the instructions God gives. In my experience, the number one reason
people do not ask for wisdom is because they think they already
know the right things to do.

Here is the problem: these solutions are often based on emotion. When we ask for wisdom, we do so not to pile it up on
top of a floppy foundation of our feelings. No, when we ask for
wisdom, we surrender our feelings, egos, pride, offenses, and
control (release every single thing) and make a clean fresh can-
vas for wisdom to paint the way. Our lives are an accumulation
of our very best thinking.

If we are stuck in a loop somewhere, that means we don't
have the breakthrough thought that will get us out of the loop.
Therefore, we have to come to a humble place where we are
okay not knowing everything and can admit we need help. We

need to stop and ask for directions! Trust me, the crazy unREST loop isn't worth holding on to our egos.

> And if anyone longs to be wise, ask God for wisdom and he will give it! He won't see your lack of wisdom as an opportunity to scold you over your failures but he will overwhelm your failures with his generous grace. (James 1:5)

Third: Feast on Peace, Not Panic

Anxiety (unREST) always demands to be fed. Its appetite is unrelenting, and it won't let you pass by without giving it a meal of some sort. If you want to battle this pig, you need a meal that will hush anxiety's growling stomach altogether.

> Though many wish to fight and the tide of battle turns against me,
> by your power I will be safe and secure;
> peace will be my portion. (Ps. 55:18)

Say this aloud: "Peace is my portion." Imagine the peace of God satisfying your appetite when your nerves run wild or you begin to desire to control people and your surroundings. See yourself taking a portion of the peace of Christ and eating it when you feel the gnawing hunger pangs of anxiety.

Jesus was with his disciples in a boat out to sea. A wild storm was raging around them, but Jesus was fast asleep in the boat. Peace was his portion. The disciples were not feeding on peace. They were feeding on fear—feasting on panic! They couldn't believe Jesus could be sleeping at a time like this.

> But Jesus was calmly sleeping in the stern, resting on a cushion. So they shook him awake, saying, "Teacher, don't you even care

that we are all about to die!" Fully awake, he rebuked the storm and shouted to the sea, "Hush! Calm down!" All at once the wind stopped howling and the water became perfectly calm.

Then he turned to his disciples and said to them, "Why are you so afraid? Haven't you learned to trust yet?" But they were overwhelmed with fear and awe and said to one another, "Who is this man who has such authority that even the wind and waves obey him?" (Mark 4:38–41)

When fear rises up in my mind and I am tossed and turned by the crashing waves of emotions, I put a hand on my heart and a hand on my head and say aloud, "Peace, be still—trust!" Try this now and see how you feel.

With the power given to us through Jesus Christ, we are able to hush the storm within by commanding our thoughts and emotions to move from fear to trust. If Jesus is in the boat (and he is), then all fear must be silenced. The God of the universe has our backs.

When I was looping the streets of Portland that night, I remember thinking I could panic. But then what? Or I could command peace over me. It occurred to me in a very logical thought that there was a way back on the freeway and I had a full tank of gas. Oh well if it took me an hour to find it. "REST, Jenny. Panic takes you backward. Peace moves you forward."

Fourth: Waiting Is RESTing

We all experience times of testing, which is normal for every human being. But God will be faithful to you. He will screen and filter the severity, nature, and timing of every test or trial you face so that you can bear it. And each test is an opportunity to trust him more, for along with every trial God has provided for you a way of escape that will bring you out of it victoriously. (1 Cor. 10:13)

Several times during our flight back from Africa this summer, our pilot's voice came over the PA system to point out flight times and geographical markers. He was quite chatty. I remember because each time he made an announcement, my movie screen would pause and display this signal:

PAINPROGRESS

"Pain progress. Yes, Lord, you are reminding me that there is progress in pain." I was so completely spaced out on this long flight that I didn't realize until later in the flight that the screen was actually saying, "PA in Progress," meaning the pilot was speaking over the PA system.

I should have known right then that God was giving me a heads-up.

We had an amazing time in Africa. One of my bucket list items was to take my kids to Africa for ministry, and another was to take them on a safari. We did both of those things. It was a dream for me on every level.

That is why it was such a shock when, within hours of getting home, something completely unexpected happened: I entered a full-blown mental tailspin. I could not remember feeling this low since before giving my life to Christ. It scared me.

What had I done, or not done, to end up so low? I searched my heart high and low. I leaned, let go, praised God . . . all the things I know to do to access REST. But the oppression that hit me was so heavy. It was as if I was playing pin the tail on my life, blindfolded and spinning. I knew then that this was a spiritual attack.

I went to my backyard and sat in the sun, desperate to feel God and feel grounded again. I had to wait on God to make his move. I didn't have any moves of my own. A picture of the message on my flight screen flashed through my mind— P A I N P R O G R E S S. "There is progress in this pain." I realized I wasn't getting myself out of this one. Somehow this would be progress for me, but oh, so painful.

The next several days felt like an eternity. I am not very good at being depressed. I like REST, so depression is extremely uncomfortable for me. God didn't rescue me from my emotions immediately, which was torture. I began thinking through my life, and a sinking feeling of a "wasted life" drifted over me. I felt as if all my efforts to make the world a better place were a joke. I couldn't find hope.

I hadn't had these terrible thoughts for years. I was broken down like a helpless hitchhiker on the side of the road with no choice but to put my thumb out and wait on God. *Where are you?*

Five days passed, and I woke up on solid ground. No circumstances in my life had changed or made me feel better. No, I literally just had to wait to be rescued.

A friend of mine asked, "What did you do to get out of it?"

My response was, "Me? Nothing. I was helpless. I had to wait for God to come get me."

Looking back, I see that God had allowed the enemy (Satan) to elbow me into a ditch. In the ditch, I was reminded that sometimes nothing I do gives me the power to find REST. In the ditch, I was given an opportunity to trust God more. Ultimately, our formulas for REST lead us to dependency on him, not on ourselves. My spirit was at the bottom of a ditch, and the only thing I had to offer was a cry for help: "Abba, come rescue me!"

I experienced only five days of feeling utterly lost. I know
that many of you have gone months and possibly years feeling
the way I've described. I've had other seasons that lasted much
longer that took on similar forms. No matter the time or the
season, we can wait on the Lord to rescue us, as seen in many
of the psalms. Waiting, too, can be RESTing.

> So cheer up! Take courage all you who love him.
> Wait for him to break through for you, all who trust in
>   him! (31:24)

> The eyes of the Lord are upon
> even the weakest worshipers who love him—
> those who wait in hope and expectation
> for the strong, steady love of God. (33:18)

> Let your love and steadfast kindness overshadow us
>   continually,
> for we trust and we wait upon you! (33:22)

> Lord, the only thing I can do is wait and put my hope
>   in you.
> I wait for your help, my God. (38:15)

> I waited and waited and waited some more,
> patiently, knowing God would come through for me.
> Then, at last, he bent down and listened to my cry. (40:1)

> My strength is found when I wait upon you.
> Watch over me, God, for you are my mountain fortress;
> you set me on high! (59:9)

> I am standing in absolute stillness, silent before the one
>   I love,

waiting as long as it takes for him to rescue me.
Only God is my Savior, and he will not fail me. (62:5)

I'm weary, exhausted with weeping.
My throat is dry, my voice is gone,
my eyes are swollen with sorrow,
and I'm waiting for you, God, to come through for me.
   (69:3)

I think it's safe to conclude that God is in the waiting.

Half the battle is won just knowing there will be a battle. Did you get that? There are battles for your REST coming, no matter how graceful you've become at finding it. Your RESTing ground will at times turn into a battleground.

Remember this so that you aren't caught off guard: no matter how good you become at entering REST, you will be shoved into a ditch every so often. Battles are coming . . . but so is he! Wait upon the Lord! He will bring progress in your pain. He will rescue you. He will break through for you. Personally, I can see the value in my waiting. This total dependence on God, when nothing else will rescue me from the pit of despair and heartache, allows my relationship to go deeper into intimacy. Waiting causes us to lean more. Waiting causes us to let go more. Waiting causes us to rely on God more than any other source of strength. What a gift pain can be.

God isn't trying to hurt us by allowing pain; he is producing fruit in us. We have two trees in our backyard that are absolutely gorgeous. They bloom large pink flowers and look like giant cotton candy poofs framing the yard. The landscapers came one day, and I looked out to see that the trees looked as bare as they could be. They were not beautiful. They were not colorful. They looked as if a thief had come in the night and stripped them down to ugly nubs. The landscaper explained that the next season would bring even more beauty because the trees had been pruned.

John 15 explains how God prunes us—to produce more through us. As our Gardener, he knows when to prune us back—to prepare us for more fruit. But in the process, we look as if we've been stripped of all beauty. We have little to nothing to show that God is moving mightily on our behalf. Could it be that during our times of waiting, he is pruning?

If you see your pain as progress, that God in his wisdom and love will turn this for your good, then you will not be subject to defeat. Put your eyes on the Rescuer. Alone, we are doomed. But in him, there is impending progress and victory.

Fifth: Come Apart or Come Apart

Yesterday I set out to write, but my insides felt agitated. I was tired from the day before. I had spoken in the morning and had attended a large business event in the evening. In fact, my entire weekend had been filled with loving on many people, which I enjoy, but now I found myself a little pooped, distracted, and stuck in a mental traffic jam. I tried to resist the dry feeling for a moment, but it was no use. My tank was empty, and I needed to fuel up.

Yes, I could have grabbed for stress as my portion and pushed my way through, but I've learned that my best thinking comes from a place of REST, not stress. Stress produces more stress. REST produces more REST.

I stepped away from the computer and went to my bedroom for a personal time-out. A few minutes later, I realized the irony of the moment. The very thing I had set out to write about, I was living out. I needed time to come apart so that I didn't come apart.

Lying on my bed, I asked the Lord, "What do I need right now?"

"You need to be held. You need to detach for a moment from all that I've assigned to you, all the people I've assigned to you, and just be held."

"Oh, that's right. I'm a sheep and you're my Good Shepherd." I whispered, "I love you. You are mighty. Your kindness never ends, and in you I have everything I need." I began getting dressed for REST.

Now, it was his turn.

"Lord, why do you love me?" Like a song you just can't get enough of, this is the question I have on repeat.

He began listing many reasons why I am worth loving. He reminded me that my value is not in doing but in being his. He gave me permission to find my value in him rather than in what I produce or don't produce for the day.

You'd think since I was writing a book on REST that I would have achieved impenetrable REST status. How is it that unREST can still be lurking and snagging me?

Jesus and his disciples often had crowds of people gather around them. Together, they served the crowds faithfully with preaching, food, and love. Sometimes, though, Jesus would pull his disciples away from the chaos to REST and simply be with him.

> There was such a swirl of activity around Jesus, with so many people coming and going, that they were unable to even eat a meal. So Jesus said to his disciples, "Come, let's take a break and find a secluded place where you can rest a while." (Mark 6:31)

Jesus is not a slave driver. He is motivated by love, and he motivates us by love. We love his people, and then he loves us back and refuels us by calling us away.

Do you know when he is calling you away? Can you discern those moments when he wants to just be with you and fill you up, apart from the crowd? This is an entirely different idea than being so stressed and in demand that we want to escape and run away. This invitation to REST feels more like an invitation to come away and be loved and refueled.

Do you know when to walk away, get away, and come apart with Jesus for a moment? Can you sense when unREST is settling in and you're being called to seclude yourself in the presence of God so that you can return or maintain your RESTing place?

Forever Dependent

Learning to be still doesn't mean that we gain a confident independence and no longer need God. It means that we become more aware that our every waking moment is dependent upon his breath, his presence, and his power. In REST, we become needier in the best way, like a child clinging to the pant leg of their mom or dad. We realize that apart from him we can do nothing and that we don't *want* to do anything apart from him.

As we learn to be still, we become so aware of God's power and strength moving through us that we become intolerant to unREST.

The more we REST in him, the more REST we experience.

Two Tornadoes

While writing this book, my daughter Esther drew me a picture and handed it to me. In the center, she had moved her pen around in a large circle several times. "God" appeared in the center of what looked like the eye of a tornado. On the edge of it, she had drawn a girl peeking in. "Lily the farmer" hovered waist deep on the outside of the eye of the tornado.

On both sides of the eye of the tornado she had drawn other tornadoes. One of them was labeled "God," and the other, which was smaller, was labeled "sin." Down the side of the paper Esther had written that Lily had to figure out which tornado to go to. I knew this drawing was more than the result of a bored moment at the kitchen island. God was telling me something, and he had Esther draw it for me.

Here is the interpretation, which I am absolutely certain God was communicating:

Lily the farmer: She represents humanity. She carries seed, which carries potential for multiplication of a crop or harvest. She has to decide which tornado to enter with her seed.

The God tornado: This tornado represents the life that God calls us to live. It dominates the much smaller tornado of sin and is where God calls us to. The eye of this tornado is projected onto a larger scale and copied onto the center of the paper.

The eye of the tornado: It is large and expansive with plenty of room for REST and stillness. REST is the fertile ground where our seeds are planted and produce a good crop.

The sin tornado: Sin also takes the shape of a tornado, but it is small and crammed full, with no room for REST. There is no REST, so there is no fertile soil for our seeds to grow in. The seeds remain dormant.

Lily: Her name is Lily because this flower is symbolic of rebirth and a restored soul after death. Lily's destiny is to be restored on this earth in a spiritual rebirth and then resurrected into the next life in heaven.

The chaos that comes with sin does not have a center. Do not be deceived—we will not find REST there. The very essence of REST is that we put down our useless and self-sabotaging ways of soothing our desires and trust in God alone to meet our deepest need to be loved. Sin is just counterfeit intimacy.

Pornography? Counterfeit intimacy.

Drugs? Counterfeit intimacy.

Drunkenness? Counterfeit intimacy.

Gossip? Counterfeit intimacy.

Lying? Counterfeit intimacy.

Abuse? Counterfeit intimacy.

Sexual abuse? Counterfeit intimacy.

Hatred? Counterfeit intimacy.

Choosing sin is choosing the exact opposite of REST. When we choose to sin, we are reaching for something other than God to fuel and fill us. I am not talking about ignorantly messing up and coming to God with a repentant heart. We can always eject ourselves from sin by turning away from it and turning toward God (which is repentance). The remorse we feel when we sin is designed to cause us to leave that sin and turn toward victory.

I am talking about the kind of sin in which we know we are rebelling against God and we refuse to back up and allow God to have this sin in us. In the sin tornado, we are most likely justifying our behavior, and as a result, we are in a miserable whiplash of sorts. The tornado of sin is small but unforgiving.

God designed us to feel remorse over sin in order to produce repentance that leads to victory. This leaves us with no regrets. But the sorrow of the world works death. (2 Cor. 7:10)

I was pulling muffins out of the oven, crouching down and reaching into the hot open door. Here came Mercy, my one-year-old, waddling with glee over to the oven to see what I was up to. She ran so quickly to the oven that I turned and yelled,

"No!" I even elbowed her slightly so she couldn't get to the hot oven door. She was very offended and pressed her eyebrows together and pouted. When we don't believe that God is ultimately good with our best interest in mind, we think that his no takes from us. It's the very opposite.

We may believe he is just a God who says no and that he doesn't want us to use our curiosity to experience things. He gave us curiosity in order for us to create wonderful things with the resources on this earth, but that curiosity can lead us into a full sprint toward a hot oven door that we have no idea is about to singe us. You see, sin burns us. It wounds us. But if we knew how much sin hurts us and how painful the healing process is, we would gladly take the elbow block from God as an act of love.

I didn't care to satisfy Mercy's curiosity in that moment. Her curiosity would have hurt her terribly. In the same way, God guides us away from sin, away from what hurts us even though we can't perceive it. God's Word (the Bible) has guidelines for right living, and they come from God's desire to protect us. I don't understand all his guidelines, but I don't need to. He is a loving and good Father, so therefore his guidance, whether I understand it or not, is ultimately for my good.

Pride says that we know as much as, or more than, God. Yikes. Let's not go down that road. He is good, and until we grasp this, we may struggle with our own ways of satisfying our curiosity.

When we understand being still, we cannot be deceived. True, genuine REST cannot be found in a replacement god. It cannot be found in self. It cannot be found in anything that God has defined as sin. Many people think God is a scrooge and just wants to take fun things away from us. No, my friends, there is no one—no one—who cares more about our well-being than God himself. Take the help.

Which tornado are you experiencing right now—the God tornado or the sin tornado? The only right answer is your honest one. Write down your thoughts.

_____

_____

_____

_____

If you have realized that you are currently in a tornado of sin, take heart! You can leave that tornado right now by your free will to choose. The great news is that Jesus defeated all sin when he died and rose again. If you have received the gift of his death and resurrection to save you, then you have a new nature to do what God wants you to do.

Before giving your life to him, you had an old sin nature. But this new nature is who you are now. We call this new nature your spirit nature—it is being built up by prayer, reading the Bible, and RESTing in God. If you need to turn away from sin and face God on a certain matter, you have the power to do this because of the power of the new nature within you.

The Bible says that when Jesus died, our old nature died, and when he defeated death and rose from the dead, our new nature came to life and resurrected within us. If you are dragging your old nature around, cut ties and drop that deadweight. Turn your heart toward God and draw on his power to enable you to leave sin once and for all.

Quenching Our Thirst

At first, you will think that you can't live without this particular thing (sin) because it's been quenching your desires for a while. It's kind of like someone deciding that they will drink water to quench their thirst, even though they have been drinking soda every time they've been thirsty for the past thirty years. We all know that soda doesn't quench our thirst—it makes us more thirsty. But if that is all you've reached for when you've been thirsty day in and day out, you may be skeptical that something else more pure and bland could satisfy you. At first, the water will be tasteless, but with each passing day, you will taste and realize the satisfaction of pure water.

Jesus said that if we drink from him, we will never thirst again. He calls himself the living water (see John 4).

Take a moment now to trade in your cheap "soda" for the satisfying drink of the presence and love of Christ. Maybe you've used overeating to quench anxiety. Maybe you've used pornography to quench nerves and stress. Whatever the cheap love is, have the courage to name it and declare it dead in your life. Then ask the Holy Spirit in worship and prayer to quench your thirst. You are going to have to take a chance that sin doesn't satisfy in the long run. Only God can truly quench your deepest longings.

REST Training through Pain Training

Is it possible that the struggles of life are a gift? I know this seems absurd, but stick with me. Could it be that when we are being irritated by storms and demands, we are being presented an opportunity to grow stronger?

Some people don't like working out because of the burn. Our muscles burn and our lungs burn. How can something that burns be good for us? Well, we know that when we place a demand on our muscles that is more than our current level of strength, our brains get the signal, "Make more muscle." In turn, our bodies build more muscle fiber and we are able to lift the object with more ease. We grow spiritually in the same way.

The demands placed on us become our training for growth.

Is it possible to enter REST when we are being terribly irritated or stretched emotionally in a storm of life? You probably guessed it . . . yes, it is. And when we master this, we experience a whole new realm of peace. Wrestling with the irritations and frustrations of life is an art that we can master. It won't happen without some practice though. Notice that REST is right in the middle of wrestling.

Remember my spin bike training? Disciplining myself to be completely present was challenging. Up until that point, I had motivated myself by counting down a clock. But now, when my muscles burned and my heart rate was thumping, I focused on breathing in and out in a very rhythmic way. Rather than thinking about all the stuff I needed to do that day or that week (or how I wished my legs didn't burn so badly), I trained my ears to pick up on the sound of my breath.

To climb into the pocket and REST my mind on the present moment, I became aware of everything I felt, heard, or saw happening in me and around me. I relaxed into the pain and refused to use anger, sadness, stress, or any other emotion to fuel me. I wanted to just be present and let my emotions express the space where God called me *beloved*.

As you allow yourself to be 100 percent present, you may think about those things that normally irritate you. But as you become fully aware of what is happening right this minute, you will find that the irritations don't seem so terrible any longer.

Water is moving through the pipes in the attic.
There is a burning sensation in my quads.
Don't panic or use anger to try to fuel you through this.
Resist the urge to label the burning as good or bad.
Breathe in the burn.
Welcome it.
Dance with it.
Feel the drips of sweat trickle down your forehead.
Breathe in.
Breathe out.
My heart rate is high, and I'm breathing rapidly.
Praise you, Lord. I breathe you in over and over with every labored breath.

Really annoying things would happen, like my shoelace coming untied. The first several times this happened, I stopped pedaling and tied it. There is nothing wrong with doing that, but one time I felt impressed to just let it be, as if it was supposed to happen.

Just REST into it.
Listen to the clicking of the shoelace on the metal frame.
Allow the sound to be what it is.
Resist the urge to label it good or bad.
Breathe in the clicking.
Dance with it.

When I first started on the bike, I found the skinny little seat very uncomfortable. "Why don't you just REST into that?" I was so accustomed and trained to fix anything and everything that was uncomfortable. I actually didn't know what would happen if I didn't fix it. Up to that point, I don't think I had practiced enduring uncomfortable things if it was within my control to fix them. For many days, I shifted all around trying to find a comfortable spot (which there isn't on those skinny seats, by the way), and my heart rate would drop because I couldn't focus until I was comfortable. Then one day I just decided to breathe in the irritations and REST into the pain.

I knew there were gel seats for bikes, but I didn't want to get one. Somehow I knew that I was supposed to let go. I know this sounds crazy. I didn't realize that I was addicted to comfort until this bike training hit my life. I became more aware than ever of how much of a control freak fixer I was. This was an entire season of Jenny letting go of control and comfort.

I wish I could explain to you the magnitude of God's grace that came upon me during the times when I finally just let go. After several months of training myself to lose control and not fix, fix, fix, I was able to enter the pocket much quicker. This pocket was absolutely heaven, and I never wanted to leave it. It sounds like I'm exaggerating when I tell you these things, but I am actually at a loss for words to describe God's presence when I turned all of myself over to him.

I would get so lost in the pocket that I would not even feel myself working, and I had a heart rate monitor on to prove that I was. My heart rate would travel between 155 and 165 beats per minute, and I felt as if I were floating.

I couldn't get over how much love and grace I could literally feel. Breathing, allowing myself to be 100 percent in sync with the moment, and letting go of fixing and controlling my environment brought me to a supernatural place. It was where God would meet me. He would share things with me that I could never think of on my own.

I was with a group of friends out of town and one of them asked me, "Where do you get all the insights you get from God?" She had noticed that I was in a new space and walking in more peace.

"Believe it or not," I said, "on a spin bike."

I began to describe to her that somehow I was able to experience the Lord's presence in a way that was unlike anything I'd ever known. With big eyes she said, "I want to do that!" I wasn't quite certain that it could be taught, but maybe it could be caught? I told her that we could connect over the phone and I would talk her through an actual ride (although I had never talked during a ride before). I didn't really know how to explain or teach someone how to get into this special place. But I told her I would try.

She went home and bought a bike. We invited another friend, and in a few days, we were on a conference call together, across the country. We did this several times a week, and more and more women began to join us, and they began to experience God in a powerful way. Nearly every ride someone would be in tears or report a miracle. One woman was a musician, and the Lord gave her songs as she rode.

This is where I have to stop and make one thing very clear. The bike itself was not the key to the presence of God. It was the REST, the pocket, where there seems to be a portal from heaven to earth that opens up. How is it that all anxiety and all physical pain completely disappeared? How is it that one friend jumped off the bike and threw all her alcohol away and walked away from drunkenness forever? One time I was given an entire children's book. I could see the pictures and the story line.

Let me explain it this way: The pocket is where you are enveloped in the love of God so completely that nothing is blocking his voice and all that he has for you. If you need healing, he has it. If you need insight, he has it. If you need an idea, he has it. If you need a restored heart, he has it.

Dance with the Pain

When I discovered I was pregnant with my fifth baby, I knew that I wanted to have her without an epidural. For me, this was a big deal because I had delivered my previous four children with all the pain meds I could get in my body. I have a low pain tolerance.

But I wanted to have this baby without pain meds. Not because I was trying to win some award. If you deliver four kids with pain meds, you sort of forfeit any future accolades for accomplishing a natural childbirth. I wanted to do it because I wanted this to be the real litmus test of working from the pocket of REST. It was like a final exam. I knew that I had to "dance" with the contractions. I had to lean into God as they came in like a semitruck full steam ahead. I would envision myself breathing in a contraction as if I were breathing in an ocean wave, allowing it to overcome me and produce its work in my body. I knew that fear would cause pain, but I had trained on the bike for this moment. Be present. Host God's presence. Honor how God made your body. Breathe in the pain. Don't fight it. Dance with it.

I had to labor to get into the pocket and invite the pain in with me. Once we were there, the RESTing place became a ballroom, and I danced with every physical and emotional pain.

I allowed the pain to do its work in me. I gave way to it and trusted God in whatever process came about. I had no expectations for myself or anyone else. Bob's only job was to love me, and that sort of didn't even matter at the time, honestly.

Throughout the labor, I danced with the pain and made it my friend. I allowed the contractions to take over. I found the pocket, pulling long breaths into my core as deeply as I could. The only thing I knew was that I was going into a tornado of contractions that had no countdown clock. I told the nurse, "I'm not in a hurry. I'm just here to let this baby come out and be present. I'm letting go of all expectations."

Mercy Evangeline came into this world in a unique way. A few nurses and doctors came into the room over the next couple of days and said, "We are calling it 'the silent birth.'" I didn't know why, and then they explained that I shut my eyes and didn't say a single word until she came out.

I didn't intend to go silent, and that's not the measure of a "perfect" birth. There is no perfect birth. A newborn baby is a perfect creation, no matter how they get here. But my story reveals that REST training is transferable.

To practice this final way of finding REST, ask yourself, Where in my life do I think that dancing with pain could perhaps be a birth of something that has been growing within me? A dream? A longing? A vision for my life? Most of my breakthroughs in life in these areas have come through a labor process that mimics the dance with labor contractions. This is what I mean by wrestling into REST. You may have to wrestle or dance with the painful parts, the irritations and frustrations, in order to settle into REST and feel them leave altogether.

Your new birth is worth the dance!

PART 3

REST IS A POSITION

18

POSITIONING OURSELVES IN REST

*N*ow that you've entered the pocket of REST, I want to identify your RESTing position.

Fix Your Eyes on Jesus, Not the Problem

A few months ago, Bob and I were having a "marriage moment," and for about two minutes, I lost perspective. I felt powerless, and my mind teetered with *Well, I suppose our relationship is going down the tubes.* I could envision my hand hovering over the panic button. At that moment, I delicately inched away from freaking out and stopped flurrying around the house. It was time to climb back into the pocket.

Stop.
Breathe.

Focus on Jesus.
God is love.
Love is here.
Now listen.

Then the Lord simply prompted me to open my journal. I flipped open to what felt like a random page, and my eyes landed on something I had written a long time ago.

A loss of perspective erodes your faith. One fight with a spouse and you think your marriage is headed for destruction; your teenager has a season of being distant and you think you've completely failed as a mom; a few losses in business and you must be doing something terribly wrong; one challenge with a friend and your relationship is over. A loss of perspective will erode your faith.

I didn't even remember writing this, but I needed to hear it again right then. I sensed a whisper in my spirit: "Zoom out." I had zoomed in so far on this one frustrating situation that I had allowed it to become the theme of my marriage as a whole. All the goodness of our relationship wasn't even in the frame of the lens because I was overly zoomed in on a moment. I was focused on a problem, not a person—Jesus is so much bigger than an argument with Bob. Never mind that I have an eighteen-year history of marriage to this amazing man and we've had hundreds of beautiful times together. It was scary how quickly a loss of perspective eroded my faith.

The pocket is the place where the goodness of God overwhelms us and we are most aware of how big God is. In light of how big God is, our problems seem so minor. The elevator music in the pocket is singing praises to God, and our senses are heightened to how sweet and loving and perfect Jesus is. We are zoomed in on Jesus and his goodness.

The pocket is the womb of the Father. It's the pouch of the mama kangaroo. A victim doesn't even believe they have a pouch or a womb or a good God to collapse into. A victim carries an orphan spirit and looks at problems as larger than life. Anxiety is the product of this person. When they pray, they mostly ask questions rather than make statements. "Why is this happening?" "When will this be over?" "Aren't you going to do something about this?"

REST is where we place great faith in our great God.

Like many people, I have a very full life. But I chose a majority of it. I chose to get married. I chose to have kids. I chose to plant a church. I chose to start a business. I chose to write a book. And you know what came with all those choices? Problems. More than I would like, but they are part of the package.

We live in a fallen world. Jesus knew that getting out of this thing without our fair share of mistakes and troubles was going to be difficult for us. Hence the reason he chose to go to the cross. Thank you, Jesus, for seeing what we were up against. Awful things happen in a world that is fallen. And therefore, it is ignorant of us to think that we deserve or should have a problem-free life. Not going to happen. Becoming a Christian doesn't mean we have fewer problems, but it does mean we have a God who is bigger than all of them put together.

Problems are proof we're still alive. I know that people settle for being stressed, anxious, depressed, worried, and alone. They write off their dreams as childish or insignificant. But Jesus came to give us life and life more abundantly (John 10:10). He came to give us joy. He came to give us peace and REST. Stress, depression, anxiety, unREST . . . these are all products of not understanding who Jesus is to us.

We're about ready to land this plane. Have you gotten to this space of faith in God? Have you done the trust fall and seen how sweet it is to transfer your focus from your problems to Jesus?

Place Your Load Next to Jesus

Jesus said that if we have heavy loads, burdens weighing us down, we can come to him and he will give REST to our souls. That's a promise! "Come next to me all you weary, picking up your loads: I am your oasis" (Matt. 11:28 ARTB).

When we are in our RESTing place, we aren't ignoring our responsibilities, challenges, and projects and just checking out for the sake of peace. No, Jesus calls us to sit next to him and bring our burdens with us. And here is the best part: he is our oasis.

An oasis? This is so exciting! An oasis is a fertile place in the middle of a desert. Are you getting this? Jesus is basically saying that he is a fertile place in the middle of our dry places. Fertility is what we want. We want things to multiply, grow, break through, and explode in our favor. We want relationships, jobs, projects, and responsibilities to flourish with fruit and goodness. This is what happens in an oasis. In a desert, they shrivel up.

Imagine "coming next to him" in the pocket. You have these things that are heavy and burdensome. They are dry and demanding. In this RESTing position, you are coming next to him and filling up on his love. As you align with his presence and love in the pocket, it becomes a place where burdens lighten, and the oasis of REST creates an environment of fertility where your life assignments can flourish, multiply, and grow. Bearing our own loads can leave us feeling as if we are dragging them through a desert. But Jesus is the oasis providing life in the middle of a dry place.

When I would get on my bike and get lost in the pocket, I would get amazing ideas for business, and creativity would pour over me. I didn't escape from my business, kids, ministry, and responsibilities. No, it was quite the opposite. The oasis was the most fertile place for ideas I never would have come up with on my own. I developed many amazing strategies for business and church while on my bike, in the REST training room.

Riding my bike was simply a training method for me to practice finding the pocket so that I could transfer what I had learned to my everyday life. Ideas and creativity from God are available to us 24/7 as we understand how to get in alignment with his presence.

Leave the Growing to God

I used to think it was up to me to make things happen. This is desert living. Exhausting! I read a Scripture passage several years ago that set me free from thinking I had to somehow control the outcome of my life assignments.

> My job was to plant the seed, and Apollos was called to water it. *Any growth comes from God*, so the ones who water and plant have nothing to brag about. *God, who causes the growth*, is the only One who matters. The one who plants is no greater than the one who waters; both will be rewarded based on their work. (1 Cor. 3:6–8 VOICE, emphasis added)

It was suddenly obvious: my job is to plant and water the assignments that God puts in my life, and God does the growing. He is the God of increase. Do you know how freeing this is? As a parent, I am to steward my kids by planting and watering truth, love, discipline, and so on, but where and how my children increase is up to God. As a business owner, my job is to plant products and serve people, but the only business activity that will multiply into a harvest is what God decides will grow.

Some may use this truth that "only God can make something grow" as an excuse to do nothing. But notice what that Scripture passage says: someone is planting and someone is watering. So there is no abracadabra about this. God uses people to work with the resources he gives. We plant and water (work) as an honor unto God. Our diligence in our work is the raw material that God uses to increase something.

We cannot make something grow, but our neglect can prevent something from growing.

My mom got into growing orchids several years ago. She explained to me that they are finicky plants and difficult to grow. They have very specific needs and can be easily overwatered or given too much sunlight. She couldn't just wing it. She studied the ins and outs of how to keep these plants alive and growing. With increase in knowledge and time, she became confident in her ability to grow orchids. More of them were able to grow and survive as she educated herself. She couldn't just plant and water haphazardly. There was a specific way to care for these fragile plants.

Although the orchids began to grow, every so often one or two plants in the bunch wouldn't budge. They had the same care as the other orchids, yet they just wouldn't grow.

What's the point of this story? Well, there are two things to learn. First, simply just planting and watering is not enough. We need to plant and water *correctly*. This is why we educate ourselves regarding the assignments God gives us. We are wise to read leadership books if we are in business. We are wise to learn about building a healthy marriage if we are married. Rather than just winging it when parenting, we should find out from successful parents who have gone before us how to navigate the parenting process. More of our orchids will survive and thrive if we are diligent and educated in our planting and watering.

Second, once we learn our planting and watering trade and have applied it to our assignment, some things still may not grow. After my mom had the confidence to grow orchids and watched several of them respond, she knew it wasn't her fault if some of them didn't grow.

I've watched people have growth in several areas of their lives and then get fixated on the few things that aren't growing. They teeter on self-pity with these withering projects or conclude that they are bad at leadership, parenting, and so on. We must celebrate the things that God is choosing to increase and thank him for that. We must keep our focus on what *is* growing. None of us have a 100 percent success rate on everything we plant and water. If we have done our due diligence to study our "plant" and give it the care and attention it needs for a season, we can REST in knowing that the growth (or nongrowth) isn't really about us. God makes things grow. We need to thank him for what is growing and take those new seeds and plant some more.

What watering and planting have you been assigned to? Are you putting yourself in a learning mode to sharpen your skill set in those areas? Have you invested ample time planting and watering? If you've done these things, you can REST in what grows and what doesn't.

Work from a Place of REST

I adore T. D. Jakes, pastor of the Potter's House Ministries and bestselling author. He said something powerful on a podcast that I was listening to recently.

"God doesn't make tables." He paused. "He makes trees."

At the time I heard this, a friend and I had been geeking out over the following revelation: Adam was made on the sixth day of creation—and because God worked for six days and RESTed on the seventh, Adam's first day on the planet was a day of REST. God made *everything* first and then RESTed. He could have made man (Adam) on day one and said, "Hey, there is a lot to do around here, so get to work." But no, God made everything, and then much like a proud party host, he pulled back the curtain for Adam and showed off all of creation. Adam showed up to a surprise party, and God yelled, "Surprise! I made this all for you!"

Adam looked at all that had been created: vegetation, oceans, birds, animals, stars, and more. Adam got to live his first day on earth (God's seventh day) in REST, to enjoy the wonder of all that God had made.

I think God made it all for Adam. And I don't think that's a stretch, because the Bible says that Adam got the directive from God to rule over all creation and to take dominion over the earth. Adam started his life in REST and was given authority before he had done anything to earn it. All his work, and ours, began from a place of REST, and we are wise to understand that we've been given authority through our faith in Jesus Christ. God was the One who had to work *toward* REST. We get to work *from* a place of REST, enjoying all that God has created for us before we ever step foot into our work.

> Then God said, "Let us make human beings in our image, to be like us. They will reign over the fish in the sea, the birds in the sky, the livestock, all the wild animals on the earth, and the small animals that scurry along the ground." (Gen. 1:26 NLT)

When it comes to work, you can REST in this: God has already created the resources you need to "make tables," and he is also the One who decides if the plant you've been tending will grow. You should feel liberated knowing this. If you're not convinced this is true, then perhaps it's time for you to experiment with it. Tend a few things that you believe God has asked you to steward—plant and water with wise counsel for that assignment—for a stretch of time. Refuse to worry about the outcome. (Reminder: no plant grows into a full crop overnight. There is a gestation time for everything that comes to life. Ask God to help you discern the timing of the assignment that you feel he wants you to do.)

Stop now and ask God to make you aware of the assignment he's set before you. You simply need to be diligent, consistent, and committed to plant and water—becoming a student of the craft. Write down the assignment along with the deliberate actions you will take to learn how to plant and water correctly. (Example: Business—I will read one leadership book per month and apply what I learn to my business.)

_____

_____

Like Adam, we've been given the whole earth as our art cabinet. What would you like to make? We are only limited by our imaginations and our willingness to learn and apply a new skill. We can REST in the fact that we can learn anything, we can imagine anything, and God will ultimately make something into what he wants it to become.

Stay Seated

> He raised us up with Christ the exalted One, and we ascended with him into the glorious perfection and authority of the heavenly realm, for we are now co-seated as one with Christ! (Eph. 2:6)

This is a great mystery: we are right here on earth, and we are also seated with Christ in the heavenly realm. I don't know if this boggles your mind like it does mine, but the Bible says that Christ is sitting at the right hand of God and that we are seated with Christ when we hand over our lives to him (Mark 16:19; Eph. 2:6).

When my household goes crazy, I appreciate when Bob rounds up the farm animals and says with calm authority, "Everybody to the living room. Family meeting."

Bob takes a seat in "his chair," while the mini people come one at a time to sit around him. Everyone is silent. They wait for him to speak. His strength and authority can be felt. He doesn't have to say a word. His sitting position has commanded the room. This is actually how the Bible describes our spirits RESTing in authority.

In prayer one day, the Lord showed me a powerful picture. I was sitting in a royal chair. It was formal and represented authority and leadership. I was sitting there with pure confidence that this was where I was supposed to be for the rest of my life.

I felt the Lord prompt me to stay seated, loving and leading, for the rest of my life. It was as if he said, "Don't get up. Ever." I felt that my spirit should stay seated in this place of authority and service to others . . . but I also knew that I would be tempted to get up and leave my RESTing place in an attempt to meddle in the tornado a bit. He was saying, "Stay seated and lead by my side. If you get anxious and intimidated by life, it is because you left this chair and your authority. I have given you authority, but it doesn't exist outside of us sitting here together."

The passage in Ephesians finally made sense to me. I was walking out my life with faith and trust and warfare, and at the same time, my spirit was seated in full authority and leadership. As a woman, I found that this put an end to questioning myself as a strong leader and minister. I could not be catcalled by the enemy to leave my position of authority for a cheap trip down insecure lane.

The enemy would taunt me with "You're not enough. You don't have what it takes." I used to fall for that and consider myself a failure at times. Even when I got invitations to talk to large audiences, I would walk away after speaking and almost immediately feel an invisible punch in the face as the enemy said, "You missed it." Pulling our eyes onto ourselves is always the goal of the enemy. Amplifying self, which is pride, will always lead to insecurity, doubts, and anxiety.

The other message I would get was "You're too much." I fell for that one for a little while too. I tried to dilute my personality into a watered-down version of myself. I was miserable. Then I realized that those two messages were conflicting: "You're not enough" and "You're too much." They were the exact opposite of each other. I realized that the enemy was trying to take away my voice by making me feel I wasn't enough and I was too much all at the same time.

In my chair, sitting down in my spirit, I felt a quiet strength come over me. This is my position. This is where I belong. Secure. Sitting with God Almighty. Leading with love in my heart for people. Leading and loving to the best of my ability—in the way Jesus would.

I heard Lisa Bevere say in a small gathering, "Strong is not wrong." This freed my spirit, and I heard the Lord tell me, "Jenny, you *are* too much . . . too much for the devil." That settled it. I was seated with Christ, and I was a strong woman. I would lead and love from a calm authority. This would be my lifelong position.

When tempted to stand up and fix or control, I would tell my spirit, "Sit down." A calm authority would come over me, and I would handle the problem with wisdom. Sitting with my Father, I would lean into him and say, "What should I do here?" He would give me very simple direction. Most of it was "love." Many times it was "forgive." And daily it was "serve." It was never complicated but always communicated that I had the strength to love others.

This last year I ordered a large "royal" chair. It has cream velvet fabric, a tall back, and gold painted trim. It is my prayer chair. When I sit in it, I imagine my spirit sitting with Christ.

Whether you have an actual chair or one in your mind, I want you to imagine you are sitting with Christ in a royal chair. You have your loads, your issues, your problems. But they are so small in comparison to this man on whom you have learned to place your highest affection. In REST, he can be trusted with your loads. He can be trusted to mend your heart, even when it's painful (and it will be!). He is the great I AM. He is the wonder of your world. He is everything you will ever need. If you have him, you have all you need. Don't look anywhere else for help or resolve. He is your help. He is your resolve. He is your oasis.

My friend Ann Hammock describes the sitting place this way. Imagine yourself sitting at the center of a seesaw. It is going up and down with life's unpredictable loads on each end. Yet you are still because you are sitting at the middle joint of the structure. You are not being jolted up and down by the loads coming and going. No, you are at the center point of the seesaw, where you remain calm, held, comforted, and led. This is your perfect alignment with Christ, and you are not being moved by the movement surrounding you. Panic? Nah. Worry? No. Throw a fit? Never. Hide? No way. Run? Not necessary. You don't need to react in any of these ways because the Father has a seat for you where nothing is moving. You are grounded and rooted in Christ—seated with him in the center of stillness.

Those situations coming and going have no access to your heart. They are just matters that you deal with in love and wisdom. You don't carry offense or pride. You surrender each moment to your Father and allow him to become the Gardener. You lean into him. You let go. There may be a storm out there, but like Jesus, you don't carry the storm into the precious space of your spirit.

A Final Blessing

May God bless you as you lie down tonight and slip into REST, into love. May God bless you as you roll out of bed tomorrow morning with a RESTing song in your heart. May you walk through your day seated, perfectly aligned with Christ, operating in his authority. May God remind you tomorrow that your position isn't running, freezing, or fighting. May God give your spirit a long sigh of relief as you put your full weight on the royal chair. May you become comfortable leaning on your Father, knowing your legs will give out if you don't. May God's supernatural grace meet you in every moment tomorrow and for the rest of your days.

Be seated in love, wisdom, and authority, my friend. You are not alone. Ever. Stay aligned with the gift of new life and with the One who gave it to you. God bless you in REST.

APPENDIX
REST TRAINING

This is an intentional training activity that you schedule two or more times per week (work your way up over time). Here are the rules of engagement.

- Choose a difficult activity—something you really don't want to do. The fact that it makes you think, *I don't want to do this*, says that you may have picked the right thing.

  - It must challenge you emotionally.
  - It must be something you would normally avoid, distract yourself while doing, or use a cheap fuel source of stress/anger/isolation/self-pity to power through. This isn't something that instigates REST.
  - It must be a beginning training activity. If you haven't exercised in ten years, for example, you may need to

start with fifteen minutes of strenuous exercise. If you are a busy bee and never sit down, maybe your best starting point is lying still for fifteen minutes and focusing only on the Lord. Take a minute to ask the Holy Spirit to lead you to the right activity. As the activity gets easier, choose the next level for you (i.e., increase time or intensity of exercise; increase silent time).

- It must be a scheduled and isolated event (something you can put on your calendar two to seven times a week).

  - Example of scheduled and isolated event (would work): thirty minutes of incline treadmill
  - Example of nonscheduled and nonisolated event (won't work): parent my overactive toddler
  - Example of scheduled and isolated event (would work): clean out and organize my closet
  - Example of nonscheduled and nonisolated event (won't work): tidy up during the day
  - Example of scheduled and isolated event (would work): lying down for thirty minutes in total silence focusing only on God
  - Example of nonscheduled and nonisolated event (won't work): thinking about God as I fit it into my day

- It must be something for your spiritual or physical benefit. (Don't choose sin to challenge yourself— there is no REST to be found in that tornado!)

I recommend exercise as your first choice—exercise that challenges you physically so that you find yourself wanting to stop early, distract yourself while doing it, or find excuses not to do it. I have found that people have the best training with a scheduled exercise activity in which they can focus on the training: stationary bike, treadmill, walking uphill, jogging, or cardio machines.

If you choose exercise and are under the care of a physician for a medical condition, get medical clearance before beginning.

If exercise isn't possible for some reason, here are some other ideas: lying totally still and disciplining your mind to stay focused on Jesus for a longer than normal period of time; taking an extended cold shower; attacking a project around the house you've been avoiding.

Do this training for as many weeks as it takes until you find the pocket of REST—that place where the activity suddenly becomes easy and you aren't fighting it anymore.

Because you chose something that is beneficial to you, you will probably see great outcomes. But don't do the activity for the outcomes. Do it to practice finding REST.

- Stay 100 percent present from one moment to the next.

  - Focus your mind on the present moment by becoming aware of all your senses: sight, smell, touch, taste, sound.
  - One of the best visuals to start with is imagining a boat being tossed in a storm. Remember the disciples and how they were panicking? Find Jesus in your mind. He's sleeping in the boat and completely at REST in the middle of the storm. Now, you may want

to imagine yourself approaching him and lying down next to him or even on his chest. Find your safety and peace in him. See yourself hushing the storm with your own voice. Become the funnel.

- Dance with the pain. This will most likely be difficult right from the start, and you may feel yourself wanting to fight, run, or go numb—depending on what your normal mode of escaping from pain looks like. This is when you just relax into it, stay with it, dance with the pain. Let the boat move you rather than trying to control it. In the case of exercise, the pain could be an intense muscle burn. Breathe in the intensity, the burning. Don't cringe or try to push the pain away mentally. Take it in. Surrender to it. Let it shape you.

- Don't use a clock as your pacifier. Wishing away the time is not REST; it is putting your REST on hold. Rest right now, not when you're done. Right here in the waves, pain, and stretching, find your REST. Relax into what you normally fight or flee from.

- Don't multitask to distract yourself. Engage. Go all in.

- When your mind drifts to the past or the future, gently pull it back to the now. Listen to your breath to connect to the present moment. Place your mind on Jesus when you do this.

- Breathe! Praise! Release!

• Breathe deep into your belly.

  - Deeply inhale into the bottom of your core (extend your belly) and exhale all the way out.

210

- Try holding a breath at the top of the inhale for just a second, then exhale.
- Count one hundred breaths and find a rhythm to your movement.

• Praise your way into the pocket.

- Fix your heart and mind on God.
- Pray, "Father, please meet me here." Inviting him to be in your space and asking for help is a form of worship because you are recognizing his nature to help.
- Set your heart quietly on praise. Meditate on all of the wonderful things he is for you. He is your best friend. Enjoy being with him in this. Find his friendship right now, with every breath. He is your protector. He is your provider. When you recall who he is, this is also worship.

• Release judgment, opinions, hurts, worries, grief, and physical strain.

- Warning: opinions and judgments steal your peace faster than anything else.
- As irritations or worries arise, don't fight them. Observe them and then release them out of your heart's grip.

  ‣ Example of judgment/opinion: *I'm sweating like a pig, and this is miserable!* Or *I'm sweating like a pig, which is good since I've been eating like one.*
  ‣ Example of an observation: as sweat is dripping down into your eyes, you think, *Oh, that's interesting. I've never felt sweat drip into my eyes before.*

- If you are wrestling with pain, irritations, or negative emotions, that's okay. REST is right in the middle of wrestle. Part of the journey is wrestling into REST.

- Completely, and I mean completely, let go of the results that you are wanting to control/achieve from the training (losing weight with exercise, getting a spouse's approval, competing with people in business, etc.). Let God reveal the results. He is the God of increase.

• Repeat, repeat, repeat! Put in the work. The Bible says we have to labor into REST (Heb. 4:11). Do it! It's so worth it!

- You may or may not feel the pocket, the RESTing place, the first few times you do this. But as you continue to put in the work, you will begin to taste moments of total exhilaration. Persist!

- This isn't something you can check off a list. It is something you create over time with practice. You will enter a deeper relationship with Christ each and every time. Don't place a demand on yourself or God to make something work. Just focus on being completely present, breathing purposefully, praising him, and letting go. Dance with the pain. Find friendship with the Holy Spirit. Have fun. Relax.

- Practice makes perfect, and the reason you practice is so that you can enter REST in your life moments day to day. The more you train, the more you will be able to work from a place of REST in the storms of life. You will stop dreading what's ahead because you know how to do all things through Christ (who is REST) and he strengthens you in this place. I am a living testimony of this.

Record your REST moments in a journal. You will have revelations and discover new dimensions of God and his relationship with you the more often you enter the pocket. After you have trained for this, you will begin to desire to live in this pocket 24/7. That is the goal—that we live and breathe and parent and work . . . from a place of REST.

Take your training moments into your day. This is the entire point of training. When you feel the boat rocking in the waves, you can enter the RESTful place with Jesus by accessing what you've been practicing in training. You will be surprised at how quickly you will access REST when you do this with intention.

I am praying that you will allow the cocoon of REST training to hem you in. I am praying that you will endure until you taste the pocket of REST to which I am referring. I am praying that when you find it, you will dwell and linger there and not be satisfied with just a small taste. I am praying that you are training for REST . . . for the rest of your life. REST training builds your wings and allows you to war from REST. Do not fear resistance and do not try to get out of anything prematurely. Let the REST in you mature to a place you can live forever!

So don't try to get out of anything prematurely. Let it do its work so you become mature and well-developed, not deficient in any way. (James 1:4 Message)

Surrender your anxiety!
Be silent and stop your striving,
and you will see that I am God.
I am the God above all the nations,
and I will be exalted
throughout the whole earth.

Psalm 46:10

NOTES

Chapter 1 Tangled

1. Henry David Thoreau, *Walden; or, Life in the Woods* (Boston: Ticknor and Fields, 1854), https://www.brainyquote.com/quotes/henry_david_thor eau_161709.

Chapter 2 Chaos

1. *Moms' Night Out*, directed by the Erwin Brothers (Birmingham, AL: TriStar Pictures, 2014).

Chapter 3 Lost

1. "Separation Anxiety," *Psychology Today*, last reviewed February 7, 2019, https://www.psychologytoday.com/ca/conditions/separation-anxiety.

Chapter 6 Darkest before Dawn

1. You can listen to this song and hear the whole story by doing an online search for Dennis Jernigan, "Daddy's Song."

Chapter 11 Way 1

1. Wikibooks, "Hebrew Roots/Trinity/Holy Spirit," last updated April 17, 2019, https://en.m.wikibooks.org/wiki/Hebrew_Roots/Trinity/Holy_Spirit.

Chapter 14 Way 4

1. Google Dictionary, s.v. "affection," August 5, 2019, https://www.google .com/search?q=defintion+of+affection.

2. See https://www.hervoicemovement.com.

Jenny L. Donnelly is an author, speaker, and business leader. She is the founder of Her Voice Movement, a national community gathered for the purpose of equipping and empowering women to live and lead biblical truth. She is a cofounder, with her husband, of The Collective Church in Portland, Oregon. They also founded Tetelestai Ministries, which develops and equips biblical leaders through online courses, conferences, and resources. She and her husband, Bob, live in Oregon with their five children.

Connect with
Jenny's Ministries!

hervoicemovement.com

tetelestaiministries.com

LET'S TALK ABOUT BOOKS

- Share or mention the book on your social media platforms. Use the hashtag **#StillBook**.

- Write a book review on your blog or on a retailer site.

- Pick up a copy for friends, family, or anyone who you think would enjoy and be challenged by its message!

- Share this message on Twitter or Instagram:
  I loved #StillBook by @JennyLDonnelly // @RevellBooks
  or on Facebook: **@JennyDonnellyspage // @RevellBooks**

- Recommend this book for your church, workplace, book club, or small group.

- Follow Revell on social media and tell us what you like.

 RevellBooks

 RevellBooks

 RevellBooks